WOMEN IN SOCIETY
A Feminist List edited by
Jo Campling

Editorial Advisory Group

Phillida Bunckle, *Victoria University, Wellington, New Zealand;* Miri
David, *South Bank University;* Leonore Davidoff, *University of Essex*
Janet Finch, *University of Lancaster;* Jalna Hanmer, *University of
Bradford;* Beverley Kingston, *University of New South Wales, Austra*
Hilary Land, *University of Bristol;* Diana Leonard, *University of Lonc
Institute of Education;* Susan Lonsdale, *South Bank University;* Jean
O'Barr, *Duke University, North Carolina, USA;* Arlene Tigar McLare
Simon Fraser University, British Columbia, Canada; Hilary Rose,
University of Bradford; Susan Sellers, *Centre D'Etudes Feminines,
Université de Paris;* Pat Thane, *Goldsmiths' College, University of
London;* Clare Ungerson, *University of Kent at Canterbury.*

The last 20 years have seen an explosion of publishing by, about and
women. This new list is designed to make a particular contribution to
this continuing process by commissioning and publishing books whic
consolidate and advance feminist research and debate in key areas in a
form suitable for students, academics and researchers but also accessi
to a broader general readership.

As far as possible, books will adopt an international perspective
incorporating comparative material from a range of countries where
this is illuminating. Above all they will be interdisciplinary, aiming t
put women's studies and feminist discussion firmly on the agenda in
subject-areas as disparate as law, literature, art and social policy.

Published

Christy Adair **Women and Dance: sylphs and sirens**
Sheila Allen and Carol Wolkowitz **Homeworking: myths and realities**
Ros Ballaster, Margaret Beetham, Elizabeth Frazer and Sandra Hebron **Women's Worlds: ideology, femininity and the woman's magazine**
Jenny Beale **Women in Ireland: voices of change**
Jennifer Breen **In Her Own Write: twentieth-century women's fiction**
Valerie Bryson **Feminist Political Theory: an introduction**
Ruth Carter and Gill Kirkup **Women in Engineering: a good place to be?**
Joan Chandler **Women without Husbands: an exploration of the margins of marriage**
Gillian Dalley **Ideologies of Caring: rethinking community and collectivism**
Emily Driver and Audrey Droisen (*editors*) **Child Sexual Abuse: feminist perspectives**
Elizabeth Ettorre **Women and Substance Use**
Elizabeth Fallaize **French Women's Writing: recent fiction**
Lesley Ferris **Acting Women: images of women in theatre**
Diana Gittins **The Family in Question: changing households and familiar ideologies**
Tuula Gordon **Feminist Mothers**
Tuula Gordon **Single Women: on the margins?**
Frances Gray **Women and Laughter**
Eileen Green, Diana Woodward and Sandra Hebron **Women's Leisure, What Leisure?**
Frances Heidensohn **Women and Crime**
Ursula King **Women and Spirituality: voices of protest and promise**
Jo Little, Linda Peake and Pat Richardson (*editors*) **Women in Cities: gender and the urban environment**
Susan Lonsdale **Women and Disability**
Mavis Maclean **Surviving Divorce: women's resources after separation**
Shelley Pennington and Belinda Westover **A Hidden Workforce: homeworkers in England, 1850–1985**
Vicky Randall **Women and Politics: an international perspective** (2nd edn)
Diane Richardson **Women, Motherhood and Childrearing**
Susan Sellers **Language and Sexual Difference: feminist writing in France**
Patricia Spallone **Beyond Conception: the new politics of reproduction**
Taking Liberties Collective **Learning the Hard Way: women's oppression and men's education**
Clare Ungerson (*editor*) **Women and Social Policy: a reader**
Kitty Warnock **Land Before Honour: Palestinian women in the Occupied Territories**
Annie Woodhouse **Fantastic Women: sex, gender and transvestism**

Women, Motherhood and Childrearing

Diane Richardson

MACMILLAN

First published 1993 by
THE MACMILLAN PRESS LTD
Houndmills, Basingstoke, Hampshire RG21 2XS
and London
Companies and representatives
throughout the world

ISBN 0–333–53493–X hardcover
ISBN 0–333–53494–8 paperback

A catalogue record for this book is available
from the British Library.

Reprinted 1994

Printed in Hong Kong

Series Standing Order

If you would like to receive future titles in this series as they are published, you can
make use of our standing order facility. To place a standing order please contact your
bookseller or, in case of difficulty, write to us at the address below with your name
and address and the name of the series. Please state with which title you wish to
begin your standing order. (If you live outside the United Kingdom we may not have
the rights for your area, in which case we will forward your order to the publisher
concerned.)

Customer Services Department, Macmillan Distribution Ltd
Houndmills, Basingstoke, Hampshire RG21 2XS, England

For Jackie

Contents

Acknowledgements

Many people contribute to make a book possible. To Val Squires, who typed the manuscript, and to the women whose accounts of motherhood I have used, my thanks for their time and their help. Thanks also to Sarah Bishop for her help with indexing. I also want to thank my other friends for their patience and understanding when my work has kept me from them. But the person I have to thank most of all is Jackie Davis, who lived with me and this book throughout its creation. For her emotional support, her valuable comments and advice during drafting and, most importantly, for sharing a wonderful sense of humour, my warmest thanks.

DIANE RICHARDSON

Introduction

Motherhood is a central fact of many women's lives. It shapes their relationship with other people, their opportunities for paid employment, their leisure activities, and their individual identities. Yet, despite this, relatively little has been written about women's experience as mothers. This is hardly surprising when one looks at popular beliefs about motherhood. That women should have babies and provide childcare is generally regarded as the norm in our society. It is 'what women do'. It is regarded as *natural*: the expression of a maternal instinct to want and care for children which all 'normal' women are deemed to possess. Against this background it is easy to see why certain questions about women's experience of motherhood have rarely been asked. Why are some of us mothers and others not? What choices do we have, and what are the consequences for us, in our own lives, of being mothers or not?

This book asks these questions. Far from seeing motherhood as women's biological destiny, it attempts to illustrate the ways in which women are channelled into mothering. It also acknowledges that the opportunities and constraints concerning motherhood will differ according to 'race', class, age and sexuality, as well as the vagaries of individual upbringing. We should also recognize that this is far from a 'strait-jacketing' process; many women have challenged prevalent notions about motherhood.

The first part of this book is concerned with how women experience motherhood. What is it like to be a modern day mother? How far does the experience of giving birth to and rearing children actually correspond to commonly held beliefs about motherhood? Why do a significant number of women find the day-to-day care of young children a predominantly frustrating and difficult experience?

Chapter 1 examines the social and economic conditions in which women nowadays are expected to raise children in Western societies, and the effects such conditions can have on how women experience becoming and being a mother. For example, in recent years the fastest-growing group in the labour market has been women with pre-school children. What effect has this increase in the number of working mothers with young children had? In the last twenty years in Britain the number of single-parent families, of whom nine-tenths are headed by women, has almost doubled. What are the implications of this for how women experience motherhood?

Apart from changing family and work patterns, economic changes have resulted in more and more women with young children being on the breadline. Government cuts in public spending have also led to a further deterioration in state provision of childcare. Again we must ask, how does this influence women in their lives as mothers?

The following two chapters trace the development of current ideas about mothers' roles through examining the advice of child-rearing experts this century. What 'experts' have told mothers about children and their responsibilities towards them has changed greatly over the years. Today's 'experts' claim to support mothers in doing what they think is best. This is a very different approach to the authoritarian style of 'experts' in the 1920s and 1930s who 'instructed' mothers on how to raise their children. Even assumptions about what is natural about motherhood have changed during this period.

Against this background of changing and, often, conflicting advice, some of the dilemmas of contemporary motherhood become more understandable. For instance, many women worry about whether they are bringing up their children the right way. Their problem is, how does one decide what is best for the baby from the wide diversity of views on childcare which exist? Similarly, the conflict between being a mother and going out to work is to a large extent based on the assumptions of childcare 'experts' about what children need and what mothers should provide.

The second part of the book examines why some of us are mothers and others not. What are the major constraints and permissions which enable and compel women either to become mothers or, in far fewer cases, to decide not to have children?

It is perhaps not difficult to understand why women should 'choose' motherhood in a society in which the efforts to socialize girls into wanting babies are so pervasive. However it is important to recognise that the social pressures to become mothers operate on women to varying degrees. For example, being childless by choice is seen as selfish in a married couple while to choose to have a child as a single heterosexual woman or as a lesbian is to invite disapproval.

Apart from the social pressures, especially on married heterosexual women, to become mothers, the decision to have children or not will also depend on the control women have over their own fertility. Not all women are physically able to have children. Also, a woman may be unable to prevent or terminate an unwanted pregnancy. The church, the law, the medical profession and the attitudes men hold towards sex influence women's ability to control their fertility through contraception, abortion and non-penetrative sex.

In recent years developments in reproductive technologies have raised important questions about women's reproductive 'choices'. Chapter 5 discusses these developments: what they are and how they affect women. It asks who controls the new technologies and who is eligible to use them? Do *in vitro* fertilization and surrogate motherhood challenge beliefs about the family and motherhood, or will the new technologies be used in ways that will strengthen women's traditional roles? Is surrogate motherhood a new form of prostitution? Will experimentation on human embryos lead to the exploitation of women as egg-breeders? What are the implications for women of being able to choose the sex of one's child? Similarly, what are the eugenic implications, in the context of present racial and class inequalities, of setting up frozen sperm and embryo banks? If the 'artificial womb' could be developed, would women be regarded as obsolete, save for a small number of 'queen bees'? Should embryos be protected by law and, if so, what are the implications for the provision of legal abortion?

It has largely been left to feminist writers to raise these kinds of questions. In the last part of the book, I will consider how feminism has responded to the issue of motherhood in a broader sense. Since the emergence of feminist movements in the late 1960s and early 1970s there has always been a concern with motherhood. The form this initially took was to acknowledge the frustrations and difficulties many women experienced in their lives as mothers, and to campaign for better childcare provision. Yet the question arises, how far has feminism paid sufficient attention to what, for many women, is a central aspect of their lives? It is certainly true that motherhood is still a comparatively unexplored area for feminist theory. This is why it is important to write a book such as this, the aim being not to provide easy (or not-so-easy) answers, but rather to tease out some of the neglected questions, and some of the contradictions, in feminist thinking. For instance: is the feminist movement right to attack the family? Why have feminists sometimes been seen as 'anti-mothers'? What role should men play in bringing up children? What are the contradictions and conflicts of being a feminist mother? What does it mean to have a son? How can we develop a feminist analysis of children's needs and childrearing practices? These are some of the questions which are raised in the Chapters 6 and 7.

Chapter 7 also examines the notion of 'anti-sexist childrearing'. Very little has so far been written on what this might involve. Here the experiences of parents who have tried to put feminist beliefs into practice are used to illustrate the issues. They also reveal some of the influences which can undermine attempts to bring up a child to be 'non-sexist'. Teachers, peers and relatives may encourage traditional interests and activities. Toy manufacturers, books, television programmes and adverts very often present children with a highly stereotyped view of what women and men are like. What can parents do about this?

Inevitably with a topic as large as this there are omissions, some of them serious ones. Researchers have in the past tended to exclude Black women from studies of 'normal' motherhood, focusing instead on Black motherhood as 'deviant', as evidenced by studies which concentrate on teenage motherhood or Black women as single parents. A great deal of the literature on motherhood also fails to discuss how class as well as 'race' impinges on family life. Studies are currently being carried out which will hopefully go some way towards bridging these gaps in the literature. Nevertheless, there is a need for further research which addresses the range of social experience of Black women as mothers, and which highlights social class differences in women's experience of motherhood.

One omission which is deliberate is a discussion of men and

children. It was not my aim to write a book about why men do or do not have children, or how they feel about and experience childcare. Although these are interesting and important questions, the focus of this book is women and children.

1

Motherhood: the contemporary experience

The experience of motherhood is highly complex. It is not just the experience of looking after and caring for a child. It is also an identity which, in our society, is necessary for full adult status as a 'normal', 'feminine' woman. To have children is to be a 'good girl' and is rewarded by social approval and social acceptance, providing of course that you are not a lesbian or unmarried.

Though not all women perceive femininity as a reward, for some its association with motherhood is an important aspect of what they get out of being a mother. They may feel a sense of security and belonging through proving to themselves and others that they are like 'other women'. They may also feel a sense of importance and maturity in becoming a 'real woman' at last. Such feelings are likely when women are strongly socialized to believe in marriage and motherhood as central to their lives and their identity, and when the alternatives for women are limited.

Another reason why some women may experience their lives as more meaningful and worthwhile once they have children, is the belief that children give purpose and stability to our selves and to our relationships. Whether they do or not, such beliefs provide another potential source of satisfaction in motherhood: the feeling that one has a reason for being.

Having a child provides us with new opportunities for personal change in other ways. Having children can bring greater vitality, fun and humour into our lives, as well as providing us with a different insight into the world. Also, having someone physically and, later, emotionally dependent on you can be rewarding if it results in feelings of being needed and wanted. This is not to say that all mothers like their children, clearly some do not; nor is it to say that the emotional rewards of having a child will be experienced immediately. Like any other relationship, the relationship between a mother and child will take time to develop.

To understand how women experience motherhood we need to consider more than just how being labelled a mother may affect a woman's self-esteem and self-identity, or how she feels about her children. We must also ask, how do women experience the work of childcare? Do they enjoy it or do they feel that looking after children is unrewarding?

Mary Boulton in her study of fifty women, married and living in London with at least one child not yet at school, found that though some women did find the work of childcare enjoyable, a high proportion did not. For these women the endless stream of daily tasks – bathing, dressing, feeding, putting their children to bed at night, tidying up after them, responding to their demands for attention – was an exhausting and predominantly frustrating and irritating experience (Boulton, 1983).

One of the reasons for women experiencing childcare in this way is the nature of the work itself. Looking after children, especially during infancy, is a tiring and demanding job which can seem unending. One study found that, on average, the time spent on the basic care of a child was round about fifty hours a week (Piachaud, 1984). Childcare is also highly repetitive work: sometimes several times a day the same activities have to be carried out. Then there is the tremendous responsibility associated with looking after a child which, because it is rarely shared and because society provides only limited support for carers, is less likely to produce feelings of self-importance and self-worth than it is of anxiety and stress.

For women who don't go out to work the rewards and pleasures of caring for children will depend on the effects on their identity and their relationships of being economically dependent, potentially isolated, and being denied social recognition for the work they do in the home. Looking after children is work which women are expected to carry out as a labour of love. It is seen as a duty, for which they can expect to receive neither wages nor a great deal of thanks. Without being told that her efforts are appreciated and valued, which infants have only a limited capacity for doing, a woman may come to feel both taken-for-granted and resentful of the fact that no one seems to recognize what she does as difficult and demanding.

Women who are in a position to be able to limit, if not entirely avoid, those things which can make childcare seem exhausting and unrewarding are more likely to get pleasure out of looking after their children. Having the help and support of a partner, family and friends, or having enough money to be able to afford to pay someone to look after one's child, are likely to make a significant difference to how burdensome the responsibility and the work of childcare seems. Similarly, having a paid job may help prevent the feeling of being isolated at home with young children, as can having a car, a telephone, or living in an area where neighbours are friendly and supportive.

Analysing motherhood in this way – as an identity, as an occupation and as a relationship – allows us to recognize that women can like motherhood but not their children or, alternatively, can like their children but neither the work involved in looking after them nor the consequences of being labelled a mother. It also helps to explain why for many women motherhood is a conflicting and, at times, a contradictory experience: one of love *and* anger, fulfilment *and* frustration.

What's the problem?

Both the assumption that women have a duty to take care of their children and the expectation that women will find motherhood naturally rewarding make it difficult for women, as mothers, openly to express feelings of dissatisfaction and disappointment, anger and frustration. Yet, as studies indicate, motherhood does appear to have negative associations for many women. George Brown and Tirril Harris, in a classic study of working-class mothers of young children living in London, found that approximately one third of the women they interviewed were clinically depressed. A close supportive relationship with a friend, an emotionally intimate relationship with a partner, and paid employment outside the home, were all factors identified as making a woman less vulnerable to depression in that setting (Brown and Harris, 1978).

Amongst those who wish to maintain the view that it is 'natural' for women to want to have and to rear children, the implication is that there must be something not quite right with a woman who reacts to motherhood negatively. One explanation is that depressed feelings after having a baby are the result of hormonal changes following the birth. Alternatively, within a psychoanalytic framework a woman's becoming depressed after childbirth has been interpreted as evidence of psychopathology, in particular as evidence of unresolved conflicts stemming from her early relationships with her own mother.

Feminism has done a great deal over the last fifteen years to challenge these kinds of individualistic accounts of women's negative experiences as mothers. Instead of blaming women's discontent and dissatisfaction with motherhood on the 'abnormal' functioning of mind or body, feminist perspectives stress that the present conditions in which women do the work of looking after and caring for children make it likely that they *will* feel unhappy and depressed.

Yet such is the power of traditional beliefs about motherhood that many women continue to blame themselves for having such feelings. Where women do interpret their dissatisfactions with motherhood in this way, as personal inadequacy, then the likelihood is that because they feel guilty they will attempt to contain and conceal how they really feel. Far from resolving anything, this is likely to make their experience of motherhood all the more unsatisfactory, by adding to the sense of frustration and resentment which they already feel.

Another way in which women may deal with their negative experiences of motherhood is to blame these on their children. In this way anger at the conditions of motherhood can become translated into anger at the child. This can be problematic for the mother as well as the child. Definitions of 'good' motherhood, which emphasize maternal self-sacrifice, and the child-centred nature of society, which frequently puts children's needs and rights before women's, mean that women can expect to receive little public support or sympathy if they blame their dissatisfactions with motherhood on their children. The effects of this are likely to be as before, that by individualising their difficulties women risk the consequences of feeling guilty and concealing how they feel.

It *is* possible for women to interpret what they don't like about being a mother in a way that allows them to perceive their frustrations and their anger as valid. However in order to do this women first need to be able to acknowledge that far from being an isolated, individualized experience, the way they feel is an understandable response to the way in which childcare is organized in our society. This way they can direct their anger not at themselves or their children, but at the conditions of modern-day motherhood. Feminism has provided support and encouragement to women in analysing their feelings in this way. Such forms of analysis also enable us to begin to distinguish between those aspects of being a mother upon which women may focus their satisfactions and their dissatisfactions.

For better or for worse

When I was a child girls were expected to view marriage and motherhood as important, if not the only goals in their life. Yet despite this I quickly learnt that such goals were not necessarily regarded as a good thing by everyone. Women I met who were married and had children frequently advised me, sometimes jokingly, sometimes not, against getting married and having children. 'Don't do it!' they warned, or at least not until I had, as they put it, 'lived a little of my own life first'. I began to associate marriage, but more especially motherhood, with a sense of loss. It seemed that having children meant giving things up: an end to a certain way of life which I might later come to regret.

This was before the emergence of the women's liberation movement. Writers such as Hannah Gavron in Britain (Gavron, 1966) and Betty Friedan in the United States (Friedan, 1963) were only just beginning to speak about women's dissatisfaction as wives and mothers. Twenty-five years later research into women's experience as mothers has confirmed what I learnt as a child: that in our society motherhood is associated with a number of important social and psychological losses.

Ann Oakley has argued that it is loss which is the key to understanding why women so very often feel unhappy and depressed after they have a baby (Oakley, 1979). Commonly expressed losses, particularly if becoming a mother involves a woman giving up her job, are loss of status, loss of independence, loss of privacy, loss of social networks, and loss of an idealized and romanticized vision of motherhood. But the biggest loss of all, Oakley claims, is the loss of personal identity and individuality.

This can be illustrated by the experience of Janet, one of a number of women I interviewed in a small-scale study of women's own accounts of motherhood (Richardson 1985). (The quotations from women given elsewhere in the book are also from this study.) Janet, who is married with two children, gave up paid employment on having her first child. After five years of full-time motherhood she decided to take a 'Saturday job'.

> My husband thought it was purely financial and he was saying, 'Oh there's not much point you going standing in a shop for eight hours on a Saturday just to earn a few pounds, what value is that!' I don't think he realised that it was the fact that I wanted to find myself again for eight hours of the week, and just *be* myself. I think he now realises how strongly I feel that I've lost *my* identity.

Women commonly experience the feeling that once they become a mother they cease to be seen by other people as anything else but a mother. This was the case with Carol, who at thirty got married and had a baby. Although she continued working full-time after the baby was born, and shared childcare jointly with her husband, Carol still found that now she was a mother she ceased to be treated as an individual in her own right.

> I suddenly found myself being treated by any section of the public in any day-to-day situation as the 'mother' and I thought how very irritating, how frustrating. It was at that point I thought, well perhaps yes, if you have a child then perhaps you've got to declare yourself more because you have an oppressive label forced on you. . . . A very important, very crucial component of this is getting over to people that if they see me as a mother that it is ridiculous to block out me as a professional woman, and if they come into contact with me as a professional woman it's ridiculous to ignore the fact that I'm a mother, because that's a huge involvement as well.

Opportunities for women who have children to maintain a sense of independent identity are limited by the assumption that motherhood is central to a woman's identity. Yet there are potential dangers for women in coming to regard motherhood in this way, as a central defining feature of who they are, especially when the childbearing period has become a much shorter part of each woman's life and fewer children are born within it. It can mean, for instance, that once her children are grown up and have left home a woman may experience a crisis of identity comparable to that experienced by many men when they are made redundant or retire. For some women this may eventually be a liberating experience, but for others who are denied access to alternative sources of purpose and self-esteem it may lead to difficulties. This was an issue raised by Gill, a married woman with two children.

For so long for girls it's been an aim to grow up, get married and have children. What then! They do it and then think, 'What am I going to do now?' especially when the children leave them. It's like the bottom dropping out of their world; they're suddenly left with perhaps twenty or thirty years of life, perhaps even more, and they've got nothing to fill it up with have they? I think our mothers . . . once they got married that was it, and now they're just left not knowing quite what to do with themselves. It's not so much the activity – I should imagine it's the void in thinking what use am I, what am I doing for anybody now, you've got no purpose in life, you can probably fill your time up, but you don't feel useful any more.

The concept of motherhood as central to adult 'feminine' identity is not the only explanation of why women are primarily defined in relation to their actual or potential maternity. Feelings of loss of individuality in women who have children are also a product of the way in which childcare is organised in our society. Women are expected to be primarily responsible for the care of their children. A responsibility which requires a woman 'to subordinate her own interests and to put the children first' (Boulton, 1983). Having the time and energy to pursue one's own interests is important in maintaining a sense of individuality and personal identity. So long as women have no one with whom they can share the responsibility for childcare (and by share I do not mean have help with), they will be likely to feel frustrated that their life and their identity are not their own anymore.

A private function

For many women the day-to-day care of young children is a lonely and isolating experience. This is partly because the home has become a much more private place than it once used to be. Not only has it become separated from the world of work and entertainment, but also there are fewer people likely to be around to talk to during the day. Smaller families, with relatives often living some distance away, and a decline in the use of domestic help (which the upper and middle classes at least had access to up until the 1930s and 1940s) has meant that women have increasingly found themselves spending more and more time alone in the home caring for children.

Changes in patterns of family and domestic life during this century have not only helped to deprive mothers of social opportunities within the home, they have also made it more difficult for them to seek company elsewhere. Servants and nannies provided upper- and middle-class mothers not only with someone to talk to during the day, but also allowed them a way of escaping from the confines of the home if and when they wanted. Also, now that families are smaller older brothers and sisters, who might once have been expected to share some of the responsibility for looking after younger children, are less likely to be available to do so.

The loss of contact with other people resulting from the decline in the use of servants, and in family size, has been made more acute by the scarcity of other forms of day-care which would allow women freedom from the home and from children. Childcare provision in Britain is appallingly inadequate, and for most women the options are very limited. Few employers or educational institutions provide crèches and State day nurseries provide nowhere near the kind of service that would adequately meet the needs of mothers of young children, more and more of whom are going out to work. In 1988 day nursery places were available for only two per cent of children under five in England and Wales (Equal Opportunities Commission, 1990).

Interestingly in 1988 the Tory government in Britain, which had previously shown little commitment to providing childcare, suddenly announced the need for it. But their concern was more about future labour markets than about women's needs. Anticipating the need to bring more women with dependent children into the workplace to fill gaps in the labour market during the nineties, the British government set up a working party to look at how childcare needs could be met. The answer they came up with was a predictable one in terms of their previous lack of commitment to childcare provision: employers should foot the bill, not the State. What this does show, however, is that governments may be willing to recognize the need for childcare provision when it suits them: when women are needed for work in times of war or labour shortages.

While the present solution to the problem of childcare for middle-class mothers may be an au pair; a nanny or a private nursery, for women who are low paid paying someone to look after their child could cost more than they earn. Women with limited financial resources to pay for childcare are more likely to be dependent on 'self-help', for example relying on friends or family, or on finding an inexpensive child-minder.

Although inadequate childcare provision is an issue affecting a majority of women in Britain, it will be experienced by Black women in a specific way because of the existence of racism and the effect this has on Black women's lives (Bryan *et al.*, 1985). In a much higher proportion of Black than of white families, women's earnings make a vital contribution to the economic survival of the family (Fuller, 1982). Black women are much less likely to be working part-time than are white women. For example 67.9 per cent of West Indian and Guyanese women and 66.2 per cent of Indian women work full-time, compared with 51.1 per cent of white women (Employment Gazette, 1987). Many Black women therefore need to leave their children with a substitute carer early in the morning or until late at night, especially if they have shift work, factory or cleaning jobs. This further limits their access to adequate childcare provision, as many council and private 'day' care facilities are not available at these times. Ethnic differences in full-time and part-time work will also have implications for the amount of time and energy women have, as well as the stresses they are likely to be under. Greater involvement in full-time work has resulted in an exhausting routine for many Black women combining childcare, paid work and household tasks.

Where a woman lives will also have an important influence on whether or not she feels socially isolated and 'trapped' in the home. Increasing urbanization has resulted in patterns of housing which have helped to destroy local communities, making it harder for people to get to know one another. For instance, the design of high-rise blocks often means that those who live in them rarely see each other. There's no waving at the windows or talking over the fence. Apart from the effects it has had on community life, increasing urbanization has also helped to make the world outside the home a more dangerous and, in many ways, a more restrictive place for children than it once was. This is partly because architects have, by and large, ignored the needs of children, and partly because the places where children used to play – streets and back-alleys, farmyards and country lanes – have become less safe. Fewer and fewer of us nowadays live in communities where children can be left to play on their own without fear of their being knocked down, not to mention the worries we might have about child sexual abuse.

The lack of facilities for children to play safely outside the home particularly affects women who live in urban districts, especially those living in poor housing conditions where there is not even a backyard, let alone a garden, for a child to play in. Tower blocks are a good example. They were clearly not designed with the needs of young children, and the people who have to care for them, in mind. For instance, the dangers of children falling off balconies, out of windows and down concrete steps, coupled very often with a lack of facilities for young children to play in safety nearby, means that mothers have to be on the alert to make sure that their children do not harm themselves or suffer a fatal injury.

Living in an environment which is both dangerous and unsuitable for young children increases the likelihood that women will experience motherhood as stressful as well as isolating. This is compounded by society's attitude to children. They are seldom welcome in places where adults go to enjoy themselves and to socialise, nor are they usually accepted in the work environment. In some cases the presence of children in a place of work or leisure is actually prohibited by law, in other instances their presence is discouraged by failing to provide for their needs. A good example of the latter is the lack of public facilities for changing and feeding infants.

The current trend towards breast feeding is due, in part, to the emergence of various middle-class campaigning groups, such as

La Leche, which have stressed the benefits of breast feeding for both mother and child. Health visitors and doctors often advise women that by breast feeding their infants they will not only provide them with proper nutrition and certain immunities, but will also encourage the process of 'bonding' to take place. (A good example of the continuing influence of Bowlby's ideas, which are discussed in the following chapter.) What is not usually acknowledged or discussed is the implications for women of different methods of feeding. Though some women may see certain advantages in breast feeding, for example it being less bother and saving them time, for others deciding that 'breast is best' can mean opportunities for getting out of the home are more restricted than if they had decided to bottle-feed. The generally negative attitudes towards women who reveal their breasts in public in order to feed an infant, in conjunction with the lack of public facilities for women to breast feed, undoubtedly deter some women from venturing far from home in case they need to give their infant a feed. This will, of course, be affected by how a woman's class and ethnic group regards female nudity.

One other possible consequence of deciding to breast feed is that it may establish a pattern for who is seen as primarily responsible for the child. For instance, with the recent emphasis on 'fatherhood' some men may want women to bottle-feed so that they can share in childcare. But given that breast feeding can be beneficial to both baby and mother, the question is in whose interests would bottle-feeding be? Arguably, if men really wanted to 'share' childcare there are lots of other things they could do (Palmer, 1989).

These are just some of the factors which help to explain why women's social contact with others may be severely limited by caring for children. What we must now ask is how, and in what ways, does this affect women's experience of motherhood?

Important differences exist in the extent to which women are likely to feel socially isolated and cut-off from the world as mothers. For one thing, opportunities to meet people are not equally available to all. This is obvious when one considers the kind of resources that are helpful in enabling a woman to have both the time, and the means, to socialise with others. Does she have a car? Has she got a phone? Are there friends and family living nearby on whom she can rely for help and support? Can she afford to pay someone to look after the children whilst she goes out? Does she have a 'supportive' relationship? For a large number of working-class women especially, the answer to many, if not all, of these questions will be no. There may also be ethnic as well as class differences. Within some sections of the Asian community, for example, cultural and language differences increase the likelihood of social isolation (Ballard, 1982).

Middle-class women, on the whole, are in a better position to get out and meet other people because they have far greater access to resources which make this possible. This will only be to their advantage, however, if they perceive the people they meet and talk with as people whose company they both desire and value. In other words, although she may not be socially isolated a woman may nevertheless feel isolated if she experiences her relationships with others as uninteresting and unfulfilling. In a similar vein we should not automatically assume that a woman who is socially isolated in the home with her children will be miserable and lonely. She may very well feel like this, though whether she does or not is likely to depend on the extent to which she regards her children as valued companions and on whether or not she likes her own company.

This last point is important. Whilst being lonely is something which, generally speaking, no-one wants to feel, being alone need not be experienced as a problem. For some women the opportunity to spend time alone may be experienced positively, as a rest from the responsibility and the rat race of a demanding job or, alternatively, as a welcome relief from the exhaustion and boredom of low-paid work.

For many women, however, being alone with their children for most of the day, with plenty of time to think if not to rest, is a problem. Not only do they feel lonely, but they may also feel afraid. This may be because, never having spent very much time on their own before having a child, they fear being alone. They may also feel anxious because, initially at least, they feel frightened of the responsibility associated with looking after a child. In this sense motherhood may be experienced as both socially and psychologically isolating. This will be particularly likely where a woman has no one with whom she can share the work and the responsibility of childcare. How likely is this?

Whose responsibility?

We know very little about the work involved in bringing up a child. This is mainly because, until recently, researchers have not considered work within the home worthy of study. But it also reflects the difficulties involved in carrying out research in this area. How does one define and measure the time spent on child-care? Many childcare tasks are carried out at the same time as other tasks, and much time may be spent on organizing childcare activities. There is also the problem of what people regard and, hence, recount as work. Is supervising children's play activities work or leisure?

To try to overcome some of these difficulties David Piachaud, in his study of fifty-five women with at least one child under the age of five, divided childcare into three different categories: basic tasks (which included activities such as feeding, washing, toileting); educational and entertaining tasks (such as reading to, playing with, and talking to a child); and indirect supervisory activity (being 'on-call'). The study was primarily concerned with the first of these, the time spent on the basic, largely inescapable tasks of childcare. As we have seen, what Piachaud found was that the total amount of time spent on such tasks was, on average, about fifty hours a week. This work was not divided equally between women and men. Mothers, some of whom went out to work, were responsible for nine out of every ten hours spent on basic care; fathers were responsible for only one in every ten (Piachaud, 1984).

Round about forty-five hours a week is a considerable amount of work, more than most people in paid employment work in a week. No wonder that most of the women said they had little or no free time from their childcare responsibilities, especially when one considers all the other household tasks that are usually carried out by women. But even if men did do as much work in the home as women, their attitudes would still be likely to differ. This is evident in the kind of remarks men very often make about the work they do in the home. They tend to regard their involvement as that of helping, and rarely take responsibility for the work they do. This responsibility for organizing what needs doing – making shopping lists, planning meals, remembering that the children are running out of clean clothes, the endless stream of 'things to be done' – men on the whole leave up to women. Not only, then, are women expected to do most of the actual work of looking after the home, the children and the man in their life, if there is one; they are also expected to organise and oversee the carrying out of this work, which is in itself tiring and time-consuming.

As long as men's involvement in work within the home is seen as 'help', women will continue to experience the emotional strain connected with being primarily responsible for childcare. These remarks apply to women of all classes, but with differential effect. For working-class women men's lack of involvement in work within the home may be relatively more important in shaping their experience of motherhood. They are likely to have access to fewer resources which help to make the work of childcare less burdensome, and which enable them to have some degree of freedom from their children and the home (for example, paid domestic help).

These expectations about responsibility for childcare remain even if women are engaged in full-time employment outside the home, despite the fact that they often have no more, sometimes less time to spend on housework and childcare than men. A study by Graeme Russell showed that the average amount of time spent by men in the day-to-day care of their children increased by just over half an hour a week, from two and a half to three hours, if the child's mother went out to work. Although the men in the study made only the barest contribution to the daily business of caring for their children, they did appear to be more willing to contribute to the lighter aspects of childcare, spending on average ten hours a week playing with their children. This was still significantly less time than that spent by the women; nor did fathers spend any more time playing with their children if their partners went out to work. (Russell, 1983). Other studies confirm the view that, despite appeals to the emergence of the 'new man', men's involvement in childcare is largely seen as supplementary (Lewis and O'Brien, 1987; Martin and Roberts, 1984; Piachaud, 1984).

Paid employment may eliminate or reduce what is for many women the worst aspects of motherhood, social isolation and loneliness. It may also help women to recover or maintain a sense of autonomy and identity beyond that of being 'just a mother'. But as we have seen, it can also mean an increase in the total number of hours a woman spends working, resulting in her having even less time to spend on her own interests.

In some cases, especially where women are bringing up children on their own, this is because there is no one else to share the responsibility for housework and childcare. In the case of women who live with men, however, the explanation seems to be that, despite the recent attention given to fatherhood and earlier claims for a more 'symmetrical and egalitarian family' (Young and Willmott, 1973), men continue to do very little of the unpaid work in the home.

If men took a more equal share in the care of their own children it would help to make motherhood a less exhausting, onerous and costly experience for women. However, an increase in men's involvement in childcare would require massive changes in the structure of society, which would enable and support the restructuring of men's attitudes that is also needed. There are various ways of doing this. At present the way in which childcare and work are organized means that there are often negative consequences for both men and women in taking time off from work to look after children (for example, loss of earnings, training and promotional prospects). This sets important limits on the extent to which, on a wide scale, men can be effectively encouraged to be more involved in the upbringing of their children. Job-sharing, more flexible working hours, better access to childcare facilities, parental leave with pay and full job protection, as well as paid leave for parental responsibilities, are all possible ways of encouraging shared parenting. Changes in women's employment opportunities would also reduce the pressures on women in heterosexual relationships to give up their jobs because, as is often the case, they earn less than men.

Not all women want men to be more involved in childrearing. In a society where women's opportunities for sources of status and power outside the home are restricted compared to men, some women may feel threatened by the idea of men encroaching on what they regard as their territory. Similarly, from a feminist perspective, it is important to recognize the potential that exists for men to increase their power and control over women (and children's) lives. It is partly for this reason that some feminists argue that, rather than getting men to take equal responsibilities for childcare, we should seek to maintain childrearing as a female preserve alongside demanding greater support and recognition for mothers. This includes the possibility of caring for children collectively.

Non-biological mothering

What do we mean when we refer to someone as being a child's 'real' mother? Do we mean the person who has most responsibility for looking after the child, or the person who went through the pregnancy and birth?

The popular image of the mother is a woman who is married with 2.4 children whom she has given birth to and takes care of. Yet in reality a child's biological mother is by no means always its social mother. Increasing numbers of women nowadays are mothers to children who are not their own, biologically speaking.

Adoption and fostering are obvious examples, but there are other situations where this happens. A lesbian couple who decide to have a child may divide the responsibility in such a way that the main carer is the woman who went through the pregnancy and birth *or* her partner. Some women share childcare with close friends, or with their mothers or sisters. Women who live in collective households may be involved in the care of several children to whom they are biologically unrelated.

Developments in reproductive technology also demand that we re-examine what we mean when we talk about a child's 'real' mother. The development of *in vitro* fertilization, for example, makes it possible for a woman to have her egg fertilized in a 'test-tube' and then transferred to the uterus of another woman – the surrogate mother – who goes through the pregnancy and birth.

So far the most commonly practised form of surrogate mother-hood is where a woman not only agrees to have the baby, but also donates the egg. After the birth the surrogate mother, who is also the genetic mother, is normally expected to hand over the child to its non-biological mother to bring up. In the United States and Britain a number of women have been paid to have children for childless couples in this way. (Surrogacy is discussed in more detail in Chapter 5, along with other aspects of reproductive technology.)

Despite these variations it is changes in family patterns over the past two decades which have perhaps had greatest impact on the number of women who are 'non-biological mothers'. With approximately one in three marriages ending in divorce, and a high rate of remarriage, a growing number of women are caring for their partner's children from a previous marriage or relationship.

Social attitudes towards women caring for children who are not their own vary. Generally speaking, women who adopt or foster a child or who become a 'stepmother' through marrying someone who already has children are socially accepted and recognised as 'mothers'. Other non-biological mothers, however, are not. This especially applies where a woman is involved in mothering another woman's child outside marriage (the collective household, for example) or without the involvement of a man (the lesbian couple, for example). What this shows is a concern with maintaining a certain type of family form rather than the biological ties of kinship. Clearly, certain forms of non-biological motherhood challenge traditional assumptions about the family. It also demonstrates that the person who cares for the child need not be the person who went through the pregnancy and birth. On this basis, why shouldn't men care for children?

Such challenges are resisted by defining motherhood as a woman's 'natural' goal in life. Central to such definitions is the view that women naturally possess the qualities demanded of caregivers; for example, a sensitivity to the needs of others and feelings of warmth and compassion. Consequently, whether she has children of her own or not, a woman 'is nevertheless expected to "mother" others as part of being a woman' (Gittins, 1985). Caring for others – sons, daughters, husbands, parents, grandchildren, friends, employers – is expected of women in a way it is not of men. Many women want and expect to provide care within the family. But others do not and, in their case, the assumption that they take on the responsibility of someone else's children may be a problem. Non-biological mothering as a choice is one thing; as an expected duty it is quite another.

Conflicts

What being a mother means will depend not only on the conditions in which women give birth to, and rear children, but also
upon the beliefs and expectations they hold about motherhood.
In a society such as ours these will vary enormously. Even within
one social class ideas and beliefs about how women conceive,
what it is like to be pregnant, how women give birth, and what
it is like to be a mother are very diverse. This is hardly surprising
when the knowledge women have about reproduction and childrearing comes from a wide variety of different sources, and where
the advice they receive is very often contradictory and conflicting.

Diversity can be seen as potentially a good thing, in allowing
greater freedom of choice, but in practice it very often leads to
women feeling anxious and uncertain about what they should or
should not do. This is exacerbated by the fact that, with smaller
families, very few women nowadays have direct experience of
caring for an infant prior to having a child of their own. Few will
have ever seen, let alone cared for, a newborn baby. It is partly
because of this lack of experience that women have become more
reliant on other people, notably upon professional 'experts', telling them how to be 'good mothers'. The problem is, how does
one decide what is best for one's baby from the wide diversity of
views on childcare which exist? Caught up in this dilemma of
wanting to do what will most benefit one's child, but not always
knowing what this is, it is not surprising that some women, particularly if it is their first child, feel both confused and anxious.

Another possible source of conflict for mothers stems from
the fact that current standards of childcare, which emphasize the
importance of play and of letting children explore freely, are at
variance with current standards of housework, which emphasise
the importance of having a clean and tidy home. Where this is
likely to cause greatest stress is among women who are committed
to maintaining high standards in both housework and childcare,
but who have only very limited resources to enable them to do
so. It is considerably easier to manage looking after children and
a home if you own an automatic washing machine, a vacuum
cleaner, can afford paid help and are able to set aside a room or
have a garden for children to play in.

The situation is further complicated by the fact that there would appear to be a double standard operating in the home. On the one hand there is the attitude that housework is boring and monotonous, a chore; whilst on the other there exists the view that caring for children is both interesting and important. Yet despite being viewed as vital and interesting – 'the most important job in the world' – caring for children, like housework, has a low status in our society. The current hypocrisy of the State adds to this, by emphasizing the importance of family life and caring in the community, without acknowledging that it is women's work and self-denial which allows this to occur. Not all women will experience these contradictions, but for those who do it is likely that staying at home in order to be a full-time mother and housewife, if only for a temporary period, will evoke conflicting feelings.

The working mother's dilemma, on the other hand, is that she is still held mainly responsible for her child's well-being. This assumption is at the heart of the concern over what women's going out to work, and their day-care choices, does to children; a concern which, as a result of such pressures, women themselves may share. Not only may this lead to feelings of self-doubt and guilt, it may also encourage in women a tendency to blame themselves for many of the problems and difficulties which befall their children. By far the greatest conflict for many women, therefore, is deciding which of these they should do: go out to work shouldering their worries of what this may do to their children, or stay at home in order to care for their children full-time?

Women, work and motherhood

To a certain extent society dictates which of these a women will do by making it difficult for women with young children to take paid employment, in particular by denying them adequate childcare facilities. Society also defines motherhood and paid employment as incompatible: if you want a child then you should be prepared to stay at home and look after her, if you want to work then you ought not to have a child. Unlike men, women are expected to choose between parenthood and paid employment or, if they have to work, to choose work which conflicts least with being a mother.

For some women being a mother is the only 'career' they want.

(Although knowing what we want is difficult to determine in a society where strong pressures exist to encourage women to stay at home and do the work of bringing up children.) For an increasing number of women, however, having a child does represent a major conflict of interests in their lives. On the one hand, they may feel that both they and their child would have a lot to gain from the time they would be able to spend together if they stayed at home. On the other hand, they may feel that these benefits are outweighed by the serious losses, for example of status, personal identity and financial independence, which they see giving up paid employment as involving. Whatever their reasons, more and more women have entered paid employment in recent years, despite the strong social pressures not to do so if they have children. In Britain, one in five women with dependent children now works full-time and twice that number work part-time (OPCS Monitor, 1990). It is now a majority of school-age children who have mothers who are in some form of paid employment. For instance, among mothers with a youngest child between five and nine years of age, 69 per cent were working in 1989 (19 per cent full-time) compared with 54 per cent in 1983 (13 per cent full-time). The fastest-growing group in the labour market, however, has been women with pre-school children: the proportion of women with children under the age of five who are in some form of paid employment rising from 14 per cent in 1965, to 24 per cent in 1985, to 41 per cent in 1989. This increase has mainly been in part-time work, which is often low-status, low-paid work without promotion and training opportunities and the benefits of sick leave, paid holidays or a pension scheme.

Obviously a woman's decision whether or not to work will be subject to many influences. How many children she has; the availability of day-care facilities; the opportunities and encouragement for women with young children to work outside the home; whether she likes her job and how much she can earn, are all likely to influence her decision. What will be most important, however, is whether or not she needs to work for financial or other reasons.

Typically the money women earn has been seen as 'pin-money', a bit extra to supplement the family income and pay for life's little luxuries. A man who works, on the other hand, is seen as the breadwinner earning a 'family wage'. This view is not only discriminatory, in assuming pay to be less important to women than to men, it is increasingly inaccurate. Although women's average earnings are still significantly less than men's, evidence of the importance of women's wages for keeping family incomes above the poverty line puts paid to the idea that women work only for 'pin-money'. In many families nowadays women are the breadwinners. It is their wages which are the major if not the only source of family income.

This is particularly true of the increasing number of women in Britain who are bringing up children on their own. Something like one in six families in Britain are single parent families, and of those approximately 90 per cent are headed by a woman (General Household Survey, 1989). There are, however, ethnic differences among women who are single parents. Afro-Caribbean women, for example, are more than five times more likely to be a single parent than white women (CSO, 1989). Such differences need to be understood in the context of racism; in particular, the impact that immigration laws have had on Black families.

Many single mothers work, many of them in part-time jobs for which they receive low wages in relation to men. It is not only women who are bringing up children on their own, however, whose earnings may have to support a family. Although the proportion of single mothers who work is much greater than mothers as a whole, paid work is often crucial to married women with children, especially if their husbands are unemployed or on low wages.

There are other reasons women give for going out to work besides needing the money. It may be that they enjoy their job and want a career, although the likelihood of a woman regarding work in this way will obviously depend upon the kind of job she does and the opportunities for promotion and training that are open to her. For the vast majority of women who are employed in relatively unskilled, low-status, low-pay occupations, going out to work represents something very different to the career aspirations of the middle classes. When one also considers the many discouragements to women with children undertaking paid work – an acute shortage of day-care facilities, for instance, coupled with the 'advice' that going out to work is likely to be damaging to their relationship with their child – one might be tempted to ask why women do it if they don't have to?

As Ann Oakley (1981) suggests, to ask such a question of women and never of men is fundamentally sexist. This is not to say that women and men necessarily construe going out to work in the same way. For reasons that I have already outlined, women may feel lonely and isolated, 'stuck at home with the kids all day', and come to view work as providing a way, perhaps the only way, of escaping the physical and social confines of the home. Another reason why women may seek paid employment is because they do not find the work they do in the home rewarding. The low status ascribed to housework, in combination with the repetitive nature of many household tasks, may in part explain why some women feel like this. Similarly, whilst motherhood is idealized, caring for children also has a low status in our society. The low self-esteem which many mothers feel reflects this, as does the low status and low pay of those employed to look after and care for children, such as nursery nurses, nannies and child-minders.

Being a mother who works can affect a woman's life in many positive ways. It can enhance her self-image and provide a sense of economic independence and a separate identity, as well as improving her relationships with the family (Sharpe, 1984). But it can also lead to conflicts and stresses. A woman may feel, for instance, that she is not doing either 'job' to her own or anybody else's satisfaction. This can lead to feelings of immense frustration, guilt and exhaustion. It can also produce a sense of personal failure and resignation at not being able to meet what in reality are very often impossible work demands.

At least part of the explanation why women, particularly middle-class ones, are at risk of perceiving as personal failure any difficulties they may have in combining the responsibilities of motherhood and a job, is the newly emergent image of woman as 'Superwoman'. From Shirley Conran to Margaret Thatcher, this is the stereotype of a woman who manages to succeed in caring for and looking after her wonderful children and beautifully well-kept home (and garden!), at the same time as doing things like being a company director and writing a best-seller, whilst still having the time to devote to 'looking good' and pursuing her many leisure interests, all *apparently* single-handed.

Ironically feminism has, in certain respects, come to be identified with such representations of women. Despite the vital role which feminism has played in drawing public attention to the

many felt dissatisfactions and difficulties associated with motherhood, the public image of the feminist movement has led to it
being blamed for making women feel guilty if they are either
unable, or unwilling, successfully to combine the responsibilities
of motherhood and a job.

That some women feel they have to cope with doing the housework, the work of childcare and holding down a job, irrespective
of whether they have the resources to do so or not, owes more
to the lack of public sympathy and support with mothers working
than it does to anything else. This is compounded by the belief
that nowadays, with modern methods of contraception, women
are free to choose whether or not they have children. For reasons
I shall discuss later, this is both over-simplified and, in many cases,
inaccurate. Nevertheless, such an assumption has encouraged the
view that women should be held responsible for the 'consequences
of their actions' as far as motherhood is concerned. This is evident
in the unsympathetic treatment women often receive if they do
'admit' to finding the demands and responsibilities of paid employment and motherhood difficult to combine. They may, for
instance, be subjected to remarks such as: 'You had it, you look
after it!' or, 'If you had wanted to go out to work then you
oughtn't to have had kids in the first place'. Or, equally unhelpful,
'Well, you know the answer, if you can't cope then don't go out
to work'.

Attitudes vary according to whether a woman is seen as having
to work to help support a family or, alternatively, is going out to
work to satisfy her own needs and interests. Although in reality
most women go out to work for a mixture of reasons, the woman
who is seen as having to work is likely to receive more public
sympathy, if not actual support, than the woman who is seen as
going out to work for her own personal gain. Where women must
work their work outside the home is seen as justified because it
is to help the family rather than to escape it. Also, because it can
be assumed that women who have to go out to work do not choose
to leave their children, it is possible to view their efforts as part
of the self-sacrifice generally expected of mothers. Women who
say they want rather than have to work, on the other hand, are
more likely to be construed as selfish than as self-sacrificing. This
becomes all the more likely in a climate of high unemployment

and poverty, where there is a persistent belief that both work and pay have a far greater importance in the lives of men than women.

Having said this, the attitude to working mothers of the British government of the 1980s would seem to be contradictory. On the one hand the government sought to attract some mothers back into paid employment, the aim being to reduce the number of people dependent on state benefits. This particularly applied to single mothers, two thirds of whom were living on state benefits. On the other hand Tory policy-makers stressed the importance of family responsibility for care, especially that of mothers for their young children.

Dependency

Many women experience a period of full-time work within the home and financial dependence after the birth of a child. While for some women this is not a problem, for others financial dependence is hard to accept. This was the case with Janet, for whom being financially dependent on her husband was a highly negative aspect of being a full-time mother.

> What I feel very inadequate about is the fact that I'm not contributing at all to the running of the home financially. I suppose it stems from having a working mother who always shared. I hate being totally dependent on my husband for anything and everything. My husband said the other night, 'Well you can handle all the financial affairs of the house,' but that's not what my feelings are, I want to contribute and I hate not being able to.

Not only do women receive very little recognition for the work they do in the home – despite the fact that it is socially vital and immensely time-consuming – they don't get paid for it either. It is unwaged work which, as housewives and mothers, women are expected to do in exchange for being 'kept' by a man who earns a 'family wage' (Land, 1982). In a society in which status is closely linked to occupation and earning power, this denies women who perform domestic work the status and sense of worth which, however minimal, getting paid for one's labour can bring. It also denies them and their children financial independence from men and from state benefits.

Whilst it might be possible to view this positively, as a relief from the anxiety and stress which earning a living can involve, for most women financial dependency represents a loss or a lack of control over their lives. Very often financial dependency means real financial hardship for women, which obviously places enormous constraints on what they can do. Women also suffer a loss of power in their relationships with others through being financially dependent.

There are those who would argue that women are not dependent on men, on the grounds that the money he gets, whether this be a wage or state benefits, belongs to both of them: not his money or her money but 'our money'. However Lee Comer (1982) argues that this 'is a comfortable middle-class myth'. There is growing evidence that while they may share the same address, family members do not necessarily share a common standard of living (Graham, 1987). Even if women who live with men did get an exactly equal share of the household income, which in many cases they do not, they would be unlikely to feel they had the same rights as men in deciding how that money should be spent.

One form this can take is the feeling that it is necessary to be given 'permission' to spend money, especially on things for oneself. This is because women frequently do not feel that the money they receive for the work they do in the home is their money, to do with as they see fit. As one married woman told me: 'When he hands you your housekeeping and your little bit extra you feel that it's not your money, it's *his* money'.

The only money a woman may be able to spend without feeling guilty is that which she spends on the children and the home. This is likely to be especially true when rates of unemployment and poverty are high. Under such social conditions the strains of family poverty are likely to fall disproportionately on the mother. It is she who is likely to go without so as to care for the rest of the family (Graham, 1987).

Some women may be able to assume that they have a right to do as they please with the money they are 'given', but this may only be because they feel they have met their end of the 'bargain', so to speak, and have 'earned their keep' through being a good housewife and mother. Put a slightly different way, what this means is that if the house is a tip, if the tea isn't on the table, if the children run wild, then the 'wage-earner' (if there is one) may feel that they have a right to complain. A right, in other words, to dictate the terms under which women receive payment for the work they do in the home.

Within the feminist movement the negative effects on women's lives of being financially dependent on men have been clearly acknowledged. The Wages for Housework Campaign, for instance, represents an attempt to get women's unpaid labour in the home recognized as work rather than as a duty which women are expected to carry out for their 'loved ones'. Analysing women's experience of motherhood in this way is useful. It draws attention to the heavy burden of responsibility and effort which is involved in bringing up a child, especially during the early years of life. But we need to be careful how far we take this. Although it is work which deserves to be recognized and financially rewarded, motherhood is not a 'job' in the usual sense of the word. It differs from waged work in a number of ways. For example, there is no fixed job description, no agreed hours and conditions of work, and no trade unions. Also, as Margaret Stacey (1981) has pointed out, viewing motherhood as work may ignore or distort certain aspects of women's experience as mothers. Their emotional relationship with their child is a distinct aspect of the experience of being a mother, even though it will be influenced by the satisfactions and dissatisfactions women experience in doing the work of childcare. Motherhood is not merely a set of chores, it is work that involves caring for loved ones and, in this sense, is unlikely to be viewed as just a job.

Apart from drawing attention to the fact that housework and childcare are work, the Wages for Housework Campaign has also demanded that women are paid for this work, rightly associating the powerlessness of women with their lack of financial independence. However money, as they say, is not everything. Whilst economic independence may be necessary for women's emancipation it does not guarantee it. It is not only through having their own money that women will come to have a greater say in how they want to live their lives, but also through breaking free from the web of beliefs which lead women to feel that they cannot do without a man. In our society, women's emotional and psychological dependence on men is strongly encouraged by the fact that not having a man, and not having his child, are both seen as representing a failure of 'femininity', that glittering prize which from an early age all women are expected to compete for and, moreover, win. This is reflected in society's treatment of women without men, noticeably lesbians and 'spinsters', who are usually portrayed highly negatively as unattractive (she can't get a man) or odd (she does not want one).

This book looks at some of the contradictions of heterosexuality and mothering for women. It also recognizes that, despite these contradictions, the family 'ideal' – of a married heterosexual couple, with a husband who goes out to work and a wife who stays at home to care for her husband and children – continues to exert a powerful influence on commonsense ideas about what is normal, as well as on the construction of social policy. In the following two chapters I will examine what has been one of the strongest supporters of this 'ideal' during this century: scientific opinion on childrearing.

2

A word of advice: childrearing manuals from 1870 to the 1950s

Most of us, if asked, would not find it too difficult to comment on how to bring up a child. Of course some people always have more to say than others, and it is likely that there would be enormous variation in the kind of advice offered. Nevertheless, the fact remains that if pressed virtually all of us would be able to find something to say on the matter. This is hardly surprising in a society which has become increasingly preoccupied with child-rearing and has built a veritable industry around advice-giving. Specialized books and magazines, shops, advisory services, television and radio programmes, courses in 'parentcraft' – these are all part and parcel of the ever-increasing commercialization of childrearing.

In many societies advice on how children should be brought up is not 'big business', nor has it always been in Western societies. Earlier generations of parents do not appear to have been subjected to an unending stream of advice and products aimed at helping them to bring up baby. During the first years of the twentieth century women's magazines contained very little about the upbringing of children; children were 'barely mentioned, save for the occasional appealing illustrations, the pattern for a christening bonnet or the recipe for a nursery pudding' (Newson and Newson, 1974, p. 55).

The content of information directed at parents has also altered dramatically over the years. Nowadays, we are concerned with the possible psychological consequences of how we treat children. This attention to the psychological development of the child is a relatively recent phenomenon: earlier generations of parents were primarily concerned with the physical survival and moral growth of their offspring. This is understandable when one considers that up until the beginning of this century a vast proportion of children died at a very early age, from either hunger or sickness. Infant mortality was generally highest among the poorest. For example, between 1839 and 1843 half the babies born to working-class mothers living in the city of Bath, England, died before they reached their fifth birthday. In middle-class homes the death rate was much lower, one in eleven (Walvin, 1982.). These figures are not difficult to understand when one considers the conditions in which many families lived: poor diet and sanitation, overwork, overcrowding and bad water supplies all contributed to high sickness and mortality rates.

More controversially, it has also been suggested that maternal indifference may have been an important cause of death in infancy. In her documentation of historical changes in how upper- and middle-class women in France treated their children, Elisabeth Badinter claims that 'it was not so much because children died like flies that mothers showed little interest in them, but rather because the mothers showed so little interest that the children died in such great numbers' (Badinter, 1981, p. 60).

What childrearing advice there was during the eighteenth and nineteenth centuries focused on the moral upbringing of the children. For instance, in Britain the evangelical teachings of John Wesley, and in America of Calvin, had an important influence on nineteenth-century childrearing literature. Accepting the notion that all children are born with an innate tendency to sin and evil, they regarded it as a parent's duty to the child to defeat the 'devil within'. Parents were advised to 'break the will of the child', by imposing strict controls. If they did not their child would surely go to hell.

Obedience to authority, in particular the authority of the father, was an important feature of family life during the nineteenth century. For a child to disobey was regarded not only as a rebellion against her parents, but also against God; clear evidence that the devil still possessed her soul. Baptism was seen as another way of driving the devil out. The task of establishing a spiritual life for the child was made more urgent by the high infant mortality rates. As there was every likelihood of a child dying at an early age, mothers were urged to teach their infants to be obedient as soon as possible to ensure for them eternal salvation. These were lessons which women were expected to have already learned in their relationship with their own parents, and with their husband, and could therefore easily pass on to their children.

A new source of knowledge

The lack of public concern over child welfare during the nineteenth century meant that, by and large, parents could treat their children as they saw fit. Not until the end of the nineteenth, and through the beginning of the twentieth century did childhood start to become a social issue, with the emergence of various campaigns for the rights of children.

Initially reformists concentrated on trying to improve the social conditions of children's lives by campaigning for, amongst other things, the abolition of child labour; the establishment of a system of education open to all; and the improvement of child health through better living conditions and medical care for mothers and infants. The emergence of a scientific interest in the child was influential in such reforms, creating new institutions and professions which today constitute the field of child welfare, developmental psychology, paediatrics and social work.

The growing influence of science during this period aided the expansion of this new source of knowledge and authority on the child. Also, since science had succeeded in providing answers to the crucial question of the physical survival of infants, it was in a powerful position to command respect in what it had to say about other matters concerning child development. This is perhaps one of the reasons why many women accepted, or at least found it difficult to disregard, the advice offered to them by childcare 'experts' in the early part of this century.

Another possible reason was the wider significance given to the maternal role by the experts. Prior to the twentieth century, ideologies about women tended to stress women's role as wife rather than mother. From the beginning of the twentieth century, however, there is an increasing emphasis on women as mothers. Women, through their actual or potential maternity, were seen as 'saviours of the race', engaged in the vital task of moulding the future generation on whom society's hopes rested. So important was this task that, apparently, mothers could no longer be trusted to carry it out on their own. They needed instructing in the proper methods of infant care by experts. In this sense, whilst it acknowledged the necessary and noble contribution women, as mothers, made to society, an emerging scientific interest in childhood also devalued women's own knowledge of infant care. The professional, usually male, expert provided a modern alternative to the old way of learning about childrearing through women friends and relatives.

This process of men telling women how to bring up children is one which, as we shall see in this and the following chapter, has been a continuous feature of childrearing advice this century. One wonders how different the history of such advice would have been if the world assumed by the childrearing experts had coincided more with the realities of the lives and circumstances of the women to whom their advice was addressed.

Various writers have in the past provided interesting accounts of the way in which scientific opinion on childrearing has altered during this century (for example, Lomax, 1978; Newson and Newson, 1974). In the main, these focused on the implications of changes in expert opinion for the way in which the needs of children have been defined, and for decisions about child welfare. Some accounts, however, have examined the way in which changes in childrearing advice may have affected women's lives (for example, Ehrenreich and English, 1979; Hardyment, 1983). The relationship between what mothers do and feel and what experts tell mothers they should do and feel is a complex one. Childrearing manuals reveal what the prevailing professional opinion was at any given time; they do not tell us what mothers thought about such advice or whether they carried it out. (Although the sales of these books provide some indication of their possible influence.) Nor are we helped in this matter by the fact that women have been consistently and, some would say, deliberately ignored by historians, the majority of whom have been men. The lives of women and children are therefore difficult to reconstruct and, despite the recent attention given to women's history, we still have only a fragmentary knowledge of how mothers treated their children in the past.

Despite the difficulties of assessing to what extent mothers translate professional opinion into practice, it remains the case that one of the most important influences on twentieth-century beliefs about motherhood and the family, against which women's actions are often judged, has been the medical and psychological discourse on childrearing. Advice on how to bring up children provides us not only with a set of guidelines for responding to children but also implies a set of social prescriptions for those who care for them. Or, to put it another way, even though books on childcare may not always reflect what actually happens in the home, they do convey certain expectations which are likely to influence what women, as the primary carers of children, both feel and do. In the remainder of this, and in the following chapter, I shall attempt to illustrate this, by considering how childrearing advice during this century may have influenced women's lives.

The importance of training

In the early decades of the twentieth century advice on infant care was largely concerned with teaching mothers how to train their infants to be obedient and well-behaved. The training methods suggested were, to a large extent, based upon the theories of child psychologists active in the new child study movement. Freud's work on infantile sexuality, published at the turn of the century, undoubtedly had some influence on the not-entirely-new emphasis on the infant as wilful and needing to be controlled. Nevertheless, it was behaviourist theories of child development which had most influence on childrearing advice during the early part of this century. The theories of the American psychologist John Watson were particularly influential. Unlike Freud, Watson believed that strict discipline and early training in sleeping, feeding, toileting and so on was the way to build a child's character. According to Watson, good habits could and should be introduced at a very early age.

> It is quite easy to start habits of day time continence when the child is from 3–5 weeks old by putting the chamber pot to the child (but at this age never on it) each time it is aroused for feeding. It is often surprising how quickly the conditional response is established if your routine is unremitting and your patience holds out. (Watson, 1928, p. 128)

Apart from lack of patience, Watson identified sentimentality as another possible reason why mothers might find it difficult rigidly to stick to a routine. To guard against temptation to 'spoil' the child by giving into its demands, Watson recommended that mothers remain objective and detached with their infants.

There is a sensible way of treating children. Treat them as though they were young adults. Dress them, bathe them with care and circumspection. Let your behaviour always be objective and kindly firm. Never hug and kiss them, never let them sit in your lap. If you must, kiss them once on the forehead, when they say goodnight. Shake hands with them in the morning. Give them a pat on the head if they have made an extraordinarily good job of a difficult task. Try it out. In a week's time you will find how easy it is to be perfectly objective with your child and at the same time kindly. You will be utterly ashamed of the mawkish, sentimental way you have been handling it. (Watson, 1928)

As always, it is difficult to know to what extent experts, in this case Watson, actually influence patterns of childcare. However it would appear that, in America especially, mothers were exposed to behaviourist ideas, both in the official child-care literature and in popular magazine articles of this period. Some authors have linked this with the wider needs of society at that time. In the context of a strong belief in the importance of the child's early years for both individual and societal development, Barbara Ehrenreich and Deirdre English may be right when they say that early twentieth-century childrearing advice, with its emphasis on the development of self-discipline and regularity of habits,

. . . seemed to offer an irresistible key to future productivity. Methods existed, or were about to be discovered, in modern psychological laboratories, for instilling workers with obedience, punctuality, and good citizenship while they were still in the cradle and long before they had ever heard of trade unions or socialism. (Ehrenreich and English, 1979, p. 187)

Mothercraft

In Britain the main child-care expert during the inter-war years was Frederick Truby King, whose ideas had an important influence on the thinking of doctors, social workers and health visitors. He too emphasised the importance of elaborate routines and schedules, but not only because he believed that this built character. As a physician, Truby King was also concerned with advising women on how to raise physically, as well as mentally, healthy children. His theories were originally based on trying to bring about a reduction in the infant death rate which, especially among the poor, was still quite high during the early part of this century. Like many others, Truby King believed that one of the most important causes of infant mortality was a lack of knowledge, especially among working-class mothers, of the proper methods of infant care.

The Mothercraft Manual by Mabel Liddiard, first published in 1923, was one of a number of books to espouse the ideas and principles of Truby King. A popular book (it has run to twelve editions, the most recent being that of 1954), it acknowledged the importance of a natural, maternal instinct in women but emphasised that this alone was no adequate basis on which to build a home and raise a family. Mothers also needed a precise knowledge of the skills of 'mothercraft'. 'Mothercraft is not a natural instinct, and the knowledge of how to care for a child must be taught and acquired by each mother separately and individually if she is to give of her best.' (Liddiard, 1954, p. ix)

According to Truby King, whilst women had a natural, maternal instinct which led them to want to have and to care for children, they did not naturally know how to bring them up. In conceptualizing motherhood in this way, as a product of both instinct and learning, Truby King could at least partially avoid the contradiction between the belief in motherhood as a natural state, and so-called experts like himself informing mothers on how to care for their infants. That this contradiction was not entirely resolved is evident in the claim that the principles of mothercraft followed closely 'the natural laws of motherhood'.

In concentrating their attention on mothercraft medical experts like Truby King tended to devalue women's knowledge regarding infant care. Both the Schools for Mothers, set up by volunteers from 1908 onwards, and the Mothercraft Training Society, which Truby King founded, set out to teach mothers how to train their infants (Lewis, 1984). In particular, they recommended that mothers breast feed their children and follow a strict feeding schedule. Mothers were told to breast feed in order to avoid the problem of contaminated milk and unhygienic feeding bottles, both of which could lead to diarrhoea – an important cause of infant death earlier this century. Mothers were also told, in the interests of health and hygiene, that they ought not to kiss or cuddle their infants too often as this was one way in which germs and diseases could be spread.

Truby King believed strongly in the importance of hygiene in saving babies' lives, and in the value of proper and regular feeding. In his opinion these were the most important aspects of childcare upon which mothers needed to be 'instructed'. Mothers were also told that to develop good habits and self-control in the child they should feed, sleep and play with their infant according to the clock rather than in response to their baby's needs. If it was time for a feed and the baby was asleep then she should be woken up and fed. Similarly, regular toilet habits were to be encouraged early. The good mother, having begun training at three months, was expected to have toilet trained her child by the time of its first birthday. Play was described as 'unwholesome pleasure', and bad habits such as thumb sucking, nail biting and that 'serious vice', masturbation, were to be stopped at all costs.

The Mothercraft Manual aimed to help mothers carry out these 'duties' by providing them not only with factual knowledge and information, but also with daily schedules for living that included precise times for waking, feeding, bathing and playing with one's infant. For example:

From Eight-Twelve Months
Feeding. 6 and 10 a.m., 2, 6 and 10 p.m.
Bathing. 8.30 a.m., top and tail.
    5.30 p.m., bath and cool sponge.
Mothering and Play. 9–10 a.m., 1–2 p.m., 4.30–5.30 p.m. In crawlers on floor out of play-pen part of the time, to enable the child to explore. Put in play-pen with toys for safety when left unguarded.
Sleep. Approximately 17–15 hours. All babies from six months should have 1–2 hours sleep in the afternoon as well as morning, in pram or cot.
Outings. Can be propped up for longer times when out, but should be laid flat when tired or sleepy.

It is difficult to know how far mothers of the twenties and thirties adopted this 'hygienist' approach to childrearing, with its taboo on tenderness and its daily timetables of instructions. Some indication is perhaps provided by the vast number of mothercraft books that were sold, as well as through the personal accounts of women who raised children during the Truby King era.

> My great misfortune was to have my babies when the feed-to-time theory was being followed. You fed your baby every four hours, not a minute earlier or a minute later. I went through agony listening to my first baby crying at four o'clock in the afternoon, and knowing I could not feed him until six o'clock. It was a universal agony we went through, made worse by our love for the babies, and the conscientious mothers suffered the most. In the same vein we were taught we must not pick up our babies if they cried when they were put to bed. We must not rock them or nurse them. We must let them cry until they went to sleep . . . (Nicholson, 1983, pp. 33–4)

Although Truby King's views on motherhood as a craft that could be learned may have been adhered to by a certain section of the British middle classes, the limited access that working-class women had to books and magazines on childcare suggests that they were more likely to rely on the advice of family and friends.

The practicalities of domestic work during the twenties and thirties also shaped women's experience of childrearing advice. With large families and no modern household equipment such as washing machines and vacuum cleaners (few homes had electricity), many women had to expend a considerable amount of time and energy in the daily grind of housework and childcare. Again this varied according to the woman's social class. Until the Second World War, many women in Britain in the upper and middle classes were relieved of a great deal of the work involved in looking after a home and children through the employment of servants and a nanny. For working-class women, who did not have access to these resources, the strict childrearing techniques they were told to follow could be regarded as being functional to their needs as busy mothers. Early toilet training, solitary child play, fixed routines for feeding and sleeping, may have helped to make their workload more manageable. Such possibilities were clearly recognised by Mrs Mary West, author of the 1914 and 1921 editions of *Infant Care*, a pamphlet published by the United States Children's Bureau and distributed to thousands of mothers.

The care of a baby is readily reduced to a system unless he is sick. Such a system is not only one of the greatest factors in keeping the baby well and in training him in a way which will be of value to him all through life, but reduces the work of the mother to the minimum and provides for her certain assured periods of rest and recreation. (US Children's Bureau, 1914/1973, p. 36)

From a different perspective, however, the childrearing literature of the twenties and thirties may have contributed to making the task of mothering more, rather than less, demanding. It represented an addition to a woman's maternal duties. Mothers were now held responsible not only for the physical and moral welfare of their children, but also for their psychological development. Also, with the greater professional interest and concern over child welfare and development came a greater potential for the social control of women. Women could expect social disapproval, the possible removal of their child and, in some cases, were liable to prosecution if they were perceived as not 'adequately' fulfilling their new maternal duties.

Such changes brought new stresses for women, in respect of the higher standards of childcare expected of them. This applied to women of all classes, but with differential effect. Working-class women had fewer resources to meet the high standards of the experts, both in terms of time and energy and their financial means. As Jane Lewis comments:

The working class family was increasingly subjected to closer supervision, first by visitors attached to voluntary organisations like the Charity Organisation Society (COS), and later by state officials, such as school attendance officers and health visitors, who attempted to exact new standards of behaviour from the working class wife in respect to domestic duties and childrearing practices.' (Lewis, 1984, p. 12)

For mothers of the twenties and thirties the establishment of a scientific approach to childrearing resulted in changes in the status and duties associated with being a mother. Further changes were to take place during the forties and fifties.

The politics of permissiveness

The new science of child psychology which had emerged in the late nineteenth century was dominated, by the late thirties and forties, by psychoanalysis. Under its influence, the earlier view of childrearing as the enforcement of a set of rules and regulations had been superseded by what has since been described as a more 'permissive' approach to childcare. This 'permissive' approach avoided making a distinction between what a baby wanted for pleasure and what a baby needed for her physical well-being. Desires were now regarded as needs in themselves. For example, if a baby cried because she wanted attention this was no longer considered an attempt by the child to impose her will on the mother, but as a legitimate need for stimulation. The message to mothers was, 'Go ahead, pick your infant up and cuddle her'. This represented a dramatic change from earlier advice, which had stressed that this kind of treatment would only spoil the child and lead to its later tyranny.

Similarly, whereas experts had previously told mothers that they must at all costs prevent their child indulging in 'bad habits' like thumb sucking or masturbation, they now advised them not to worry. Such behaviour was merely a part of the child's need to explore and learn about the world. To stop them, all one had to do was provide an alternative object of interest to explore. If this failed then better to let the behaviour wane of its own accord than worry about trying to stop it. To worry would most likely only make the situation worse by making the child anxious or guilty, thus prolonging the undesired behaviour.

Thumbsucking, unless very prolonged, leads to no ill-effects to the mouth or the teeth, and masturbation has no unpleasant or dangerous consequences. They are tried out by almost every child for a while and found more or less pleasurable. For that reason they may be indulged in when there is nothing better to do . . . A child can safely be left to suck his thumb in moderation. If he is doing so excessively he can usually be weaned off the habit more successfully by gently removing his hand from his mouth and offering him some more interesting activity, than by any forcible means of prevention. In the same way the little boy or little girl who begins to masturbate can be allowed to do so without any harm and will usually soon give up the practice of his or her own accord. If it becomes a habit, gentle correction and diversion of attention are all that is necessary. (Moncrief, 1948, pp. 188–90)

This shift away from authoritarian advice on childrearing, with its emphasis on control, to a more permissive approach, which allowed a certain amount of indulgence, had important implications for what were considered to be the nature and extent of a woman's maternal duties. According to the experts of the forties and fifties, babies no longer needed mothers to provide a constant check on their bad habits but instead to meet their needs for stimulation whenever or wherever such needs might occur. Expert opinion was far less concerned with informing women about physical care, than it was about emphasizing and enlarging upon those aspects of care identified as being crucial to the psychological well-being of the child. Mothers had new responsibilities to their children: it was on them that the child's intellectual, social and emotional development depended.

Educationalists, influenced by the work of Jean Piaget and by psychoanalytic writers such as Susan Isaacs, were beginning to recognize the importance of the mother playing with her infant. Whereas previously play had been regarded as a means for 'unwholesome pleasure', it was now considered vitally important for future intellectual and social development. Play was the process whereby the child explored her world and came to understand it. From the point of view of the mother play was not only permissible but a requirement, a new maternal duty. Martha Wolfenstein refers to this as the 'fun morality' of the forties and fifties: the moral obligation to 'simply' enjoy one's child (Wolfenstein, 1955).

From initially focusing on what the child did, the experts had become more concerned with the mother's attitude towards what her child was doing. It was the mother's emotional state, the frame of mind in which she responded to her infant rather than the specific practices she employed, that was now considered most important. The psychoanalytically inspired advice of the forties had also shifted from earlier approaches, with their 'taboo on tenderness', in the emphasis it placed on the importance of mother love for the normal, natural development of the child. Whereas previously mothers had been advised to adopt a detached, almost clinical attitude towards their infants, they were now informed of the crucial importance of a close, warm relationship between mother and infant in which both found satisfaction and enjoyment. In demanding that mothers love their children experts contributed to an idealized view of the good mother, as someone who unselfishly and willingly gave of her time and energy in order to try to meet her child's needs for nurture and stimulation. This view of permissive motherhood represented an important change in the way experts regarded the rights of the mother and the rights of the child. Whereas the childrearing manuals of the twenties and thirties had indicated a mutuality of interest, by the forties the rights and responsibilities of mothers were increasingly being defined in terms of what the child needed of them. Women had lost a certain amount of independence within the mother–child relationship; the needs and wants of the child were now expected to take precedence over those of the mother. As Nancy Pottishman Weiss remarked: 'In the first editions of Infant Care what was good for the mother was good for the child. By World War II, what benefited the child was not necessarily in the mother's best interests' (Weiss, 1978, p. 39).

For the psychoanalytically inspired advocates of permissive childrearing, what benefited the child *was* in the mother's best interests. The good mother was a woman whose psychosexual maturity was expressed in her desire for motherhood, and who found her own fulfilment in meeting her child's needs.

Psychoanalysts like Margaret Ribble in the United States, and John Bowlby and Donald Winnicott in England, supported this view of motherhood. Yet despite the widespread influence of their ideas, which are discussed in the following chapter, it is the name Benjamin Spock which has become synonymous with the permissive approach to childrearing. His book *Baby and Child Care*, first published in 1946, has sold millions of copies. Though it reflected the views of psychoanalysts like Ribble, Winnicott and Bowlby, it was written in a much more accessible style. This may, in part, account for Spock's popularity. However, we still need to ask why such descriptions of mothering attracted the attention they did during the forties and fifties?

In one sense it is easy to see how permissiveness could be regarded by mothers as an improvement on previous advice. The old authoritarian approach, which instructed mothers on how they ought to bring up their children, had been superseded by advice which stressed flexibility rather than a rigid routine. The decreased emphasis on specific techniques aimed at controlling the child was, in some senses, more permissive for both mother and child, in terms of what they should or should not do. Mothers were allowed to express their love for their infant (indeed, they were expected to), and the child could be indulged. The advice mothers received was also couched in a language that was both less stern and formal than it had been previously.

The popularity of books like *Baby and Child Care* cannot, however, be entirely explained in terms of a reaction against the authoritarian advice of the twenties and thirties. As with earlier approaches to childrearing, it is possible to link the popularity of permissive advice to the wider needs of society. Permissiveness, it has been argued, suited the requirements of the new consumer society with its emphasis on individual consumption. Although the following remarks by Barbara Ehrenreich and Deirdre English specifically refer to the United States, where the process of consumerism occurred slightly earlier and to a somewhat greater extent than it did elsewhere, we can apply their analysis to Britain in the late fifties and early sixties.

In the broadest sense, permissiveness was much more than child raising – it was like a national mood, a kind of change which swept through everything. The American economy was becoming more and more dependent on individual consumption – of cars, housing, and an ever-expanding panoply of domestic goods – and the ethos of permissiveness flourished in the climate of consumption. The experts who had been concerned with discipline and self-control now discovered that self-indulgence was healthy for the individual personality just as it was good for the entire economy. (Ehrenreich and English, 1979, p. 191)

The discovery that self-indulgence is good for you suggests a contradiction in expert thinking. How could mothers be expected to engage in healthy self-indulgence, whilst at the same time satisfying the ideal of permissive motherhood with its emphasis on maternal self-sacrifice? This apparent contradiction was successfully avoided by theorising motherhood as personal enjoyment and fulfilment for women. The form that this took was a definition of the mother's relationship with her child as 'fun', and the construction of the mother as someone who was *naturally* most fulfilled and gratified through caring for and indulging her child.

In considering the permissive advice of the forties and fifties the important question to ask is for whom was it permissive? For infants certainly, although the earlier view that 'permissive indulgence' would spoil the child did not disappear completely. The so-called rebellious nature of British and American youth during the late fifties and the sixties has often been blamed on permissive approaches to childrearing; and Spock has been widely criticized (along with 'permissive' mothers) for producing a generation that was both irresponsible and lacking in self-discipline.

By contrast, the possible negative consequences of permissive advice for mothers has evoked little comment. Yet they certainly exist. For example, while there is far less concern with advising women about physical nurturance and ways of controlling their infants, those aspects of care associated with the psychological well-being of the child are increasingly emphasized and enlarged upon. In the permissive literature the maternal role is laden with new significance. It is the mother who is responsible for the child's intellectual growth, emotional adjustment, and chances of future happiness in relationships. The importance of the mother's influence on the child increases considerably in this new job description of motherhood, but she also becomes a more blameworthy person. It is, increasingly, her fault if things go wrong. For mothers the costs of permissiveness were a reinterpretation and an expansion of their maternal obligations and responsibilities, coupled with a loss of certain rights in their relationship with their child.

What also emerges in the permissive literature is a striking lack of attention to the real-life problems of caring for children. The difficulties women may experience as mothers are ignored in the emphasis on enjoying one's infant. During the fifties this process of idealizing motherhood reached its peak and, as we shall see, incurred further costs for women in their role as mothers.

3

Mother knows best: theories of childrearing since the Second World War

Bowlby's influence

The 1950s are well known for their concern with motherhood. Though the family was a preoccupation all through the war years, from 1945 onwards there emerged a particularly intense concentration on the mother which has since become closely identified with the work of one man in particular, John Bowlby.

Bowlby's ideas about motherhood and child care reached a wide audience during the fifties with the publication of *Child Care and the Growth of Love*. This popular paperback was based on an earlier report on the effects of institutionalization on children, which Bowlby had been asked to submit to the World Health Organization (Bowlby, 1951). In this report, and in *Child Care and the Growth of Love*, Bowlby argued that the early attachments, or bonds, a child forms are crucial to her future mental health. He qualified this by saying that it is the child's attachment to the mother which is essential; other attachments he claimed were less important. Bowlby implicitly accepted traditional beliefs about the role of women and men within the family. The role of the father was, he claimed, to enable the mother to devote herself to the constant care of her child, through the provision of economic and emotional support (Bowlby, 1953).

In order that the process of maternal bonding could take place Bowlby argued that the child needed to experience a warm, intimate and continuous relationship with the mother, in which both found satisfaction and enjoyment. In this, and in other respects, Bowlby emphasized the emotional aspects of the mother's

43

relationship with the child. Being a good mother meant adopting a positive and loving attitude towards one's infant. All a mother had to do to achieve this was just to act naturally. For instance, according to Bowlby, providing she spends time getting to know and understand her infant 'the normal mother can afford to rely on the prompting of her instincts in the happy knowledge that the tenderness they prompt is what her baby wants' (Bowlby, 1953, p. 20). Similarly, in discussing children who have been severely deprived of 'normal' maternal love and care during infancy, Bowlby states that '. . . it is exactly the kind of care which a mother gives without thinking that is the care which they have lacked' (Bowlby, 1953, p. 18).

This represented a redefinition of what was assumed to come naturally to mothers. Maternal instinct can be defined as knowing instinctively how to look after and care for a child; as a natural desire to have children; as an instinctive love for one's child; or as a combination of these. Childrearing advice of the 1920s and 1930s suggested that whilst it was natural for women to want to have a child and to look after it, mothers did not necessarily know instinctively what was best for their infant. They had to acquire the skills and the knowledge of childcare from experts like Truby King. For the psychoanalytically orientated experts of the forties and fifties, the concept of maternal instinct incorporated all of these three elements. Education for motherhood was seen as unnecessary, possibly even dangerous. Mothers did know best; although it seemed they still needed experts to tell them 'what it all meant', and to help in cases where women were 'repressing their natural instincts' (Winnicott, 1964).

Donald Winnicott's ideas also reached a wide audience during the forties and fifties. A paediatrician and psychoanalyst, Winnicott's views were popularized in women's magazines, and in 1944 he recorded a series of wartime broadcasts to mothers for the British Broadcasting Corporation. Winnicott too emphasized the vital importance of the child's relationship with the mother. In *The Child, the Family, and the Outside World*, which he based largely on the talks broadcast by the BBC, Winnicott declared that 'the foundation of the health of the human being is laid by you [the mother] in the baby's first weeks and months' (Winnicott, 1964, p. 16). Like Bowlby, he argued that mothers knew naturally how to respond to their infants.

You found yourself concerned with management of the baby's body, and you liked it to be so. You knew just how to pick the baby up, how to put the baby down, and how to leave well alone, letting the cot act for you; and you had learnt how to arrange the clothes for comfort and for preserving the baby's natural warmth. Indeed, you knew all this when you were a little girl and played with dolls. And then there were special times when you did definite things, feeding, bathing, changing napkins, and cuddling. Sometimes the urine trickled down the apron or went right through and soaked you as if you yourself had let slip, and you didn't mind. In fact by these things you could have known you were a woman, and an ordinary devoted mother. (Winnicott, 1964, p. 16)

'Ordinary' mothers were thus told not only how good and devoted they were (or should be), but also that they did not need to read books about childcare in order to become this. The expectation is that a woman becomes an ordinary devoted mother just by being herself.

According to Winnicott one of the things the ordinarily devoted mother 'knows without being told' is that during her child's development 'nothing must interfere with the continuity of the relationship between the child and herself' (Winnicott, 1964, p. 109). *Naturally* it was those mothers who 'intuitively' remained at home and did not work whom he regarded as being best able to fulfil their children's needs, as well as satisfying their own deepest instincts in the process. Women who worked outside the home, whatever the reason, were depriving both their children and themselves.

Bowlby and Winnicott's ideas about the dangers of separation were not entirely new. During the thirties and forties a great deal was written about the deleterious effects of an institutionalized upbringing, which Bowlby made use of in developing his theory of maternal deprivation. But by the fifties it was no longer children who were orphaned or separated from their mothers and living in institutions who were at the centre of discussions about separation. There was a new focus of interest: the everyday separation experiences of 'ordinary' mothers and their children. The emphasis had shifted away from a consideration of the damaging effects of institutionalized care, towards a greater stress on the dangers to children of mothers going out to work.

On the face of it it might appear that developments within psychology had contributed very neatly to the government's policies on childcare, which led to the rapid decline in the provision of day nurseries at the end of the Second World War. Yet the belief that the postwar government in Britain used Bowlby's ideas to drive women out of their jobs and back into the home is both inaccurate and oversimplified (Riley, 1983a). Women did not immediately withdraw from work *en masse* after 1945, nor did the government argue for the closure of war nurseries on the basis that they were emotionally damaging to children, but on the grounds that there was no need for them any more. They had been a war service and now the war was over. The expectation was that women would want to return to the home rather than continue working.

Whether such governmental thinking accurately reflected the way women felt is a different matter. It is true there were good reasons why women might not have wanted to go on working, low pay and a lack of day care for example. It is also the case that women were encouraged to view their work as part of the war effort and therefore temporary, to end when the war ended. Yet the appeal that home and family may have had for women in the postwar years cannot be explained entirely by this. Fuelled by the postwar concern with what was considered to be a dangerously low birthrate, women were subjected to a good deal of rhetoric about the importance of maternity and the significance of the role of women within the family as homemakers and mothers. Motherhood, it was stressed, was an important job. Women, as housewives and mothers, did real and vital work.

The aim was to encourage women to have more children by making motherhood seem more attractive. Further encouragement existed in the form of attempts to make motherhood seem easier for women. The assumption was that if the life of housewives and mothers could be made easier, by reducing the amount of work and the worry associated with childcare, women would be more likely to have children. The suggestions that were made included homes for tired housewives; after-school play centres; family tickets on trains; holidays on the social services for poorer families; and a retention of the wartime nurseries (Riley, 1983a). Advertisements of that period also emphasized the 'labour saving' features of household products.

Bowlby's ideas were an important aspect of this postwar encouragement of maternity and a return of women to the home. His work also encouraged and supported the rapid growth of child welfare movements during the fifties and their concern with the social consequences of 'bad mothering', which included mothers working. It also provided a basis for informing psychiatric, paediatric, and social work thinking and practice. For instance, the importance of the mother–child bond, and of providing a secure and consistent attachment in infancy, was broadly accepted by most practising social workers during the fifties (Davies, 1981).

This is a situation which has not altogether changed. Despite the serious criticisms that have been made of it (for example, Rutter, 1981; Sluckin, Herbert and Herbert, 1983), and Bowlby's own revisions, maternal deprivation theory still underpins much of what is taken for granted about childrearing and the role of women in society. It also continues to exert an important influence on the thinking of social policy makers and the childcare professions.

Apart from its role in policy and practice decisions, expert opinion during the fifties exerted other, more subtle, influences on women's experience of motherhood through the prescriptions it laid down for 'good mothering'. Both Bowlby and Winnicott minimized the role of conscious control in mothering. In their view, whether a woman was a good or a bad mother depended less on her personal experience and knowledge of bringing up children than on the strength of her instinctual feelings towards her infant. Successful mothering was removed from the control of the child's mother and placed firmly and squarely in the hands of Mother Nature.

Such appeals to nature, though they may have helped to reinstate the mother as the natural expert on childrearing, did have their drawbacks. For example, although Bowlby and Winnicott emphasized the vital importance of the mother's role in the early years, they did not always specify what it was that they thought a mother should do in day-to-day situations. For some women being told that 'mother knows best' may have been as unrealistic as the earlier expectation that mothers should follow a set routine. If a woman had very little experience of caring for children prior to having a child of her own, and if her feelings were not as she had been led to imagine, she may have felt guilty or confused when the experts told her to do what *she* thought was right.

We might also ask, 'Which is the more difficult to live up to: being a strict disciplinarian and keeper of regular routines, or a continual source of love and affection?' Or, to put it a different way, 'Which is the more difficult to control, one's behaviour or one's mood?' To fail to carry out certain childrearing practices is failure of one kind; not to feel instinctively close and warm to one's infant is personal failure of quite a different order. It is not through ignorance, lack of resources or staying power that a woman was deemed to have failed, but because for her – as Bowlby put it – 'nature's gifts were lacking'. For the woman who did not feel 'instinctively' close and warm to her baby; the woman who often felt tired, irritated, impatient or even cross with her infant; the woman who felt no compulsion to stay at home and look after her child but who preferred to go out to work; failure to be a good mother was identified as entirely her own, a problem of her incomplete nature.

Yet it would be wrong to see Bowlby's influence as entirely negative. There was much in his work, and that of his colleagues, which may have appealed to women in the fifties. For instance, the significance and importance attached to motherhood (as in the early part of this century) not only gave mothers elevated status, it also emphasized that women had special kinds of knowledge and abilities that men did not. The emphasis on the joys of motherhood and the importance of love may also have had a strong appeal in the wake of the hardships of war (Wilson, 1980).

During the late sixties and seventies feminists were quick to declare Bowlby's work oppressive to women (see Chapter 6). In the fifties, however, many feminists accepted the emphasis on women's traditional role within the family, seeking to improve the welfare of mothers and their children and to raise the status of homemaking (Banks, 1981). This limited the extent to which Bowlby's work could be regarded as anti-feminist. After all, Bowlby had himself argued for greater support for mothers through improved child guidance services, increased family allowances and more trained psychiatric workers (Bowlby, 1953).

Nevertheless, there were some writers who regarded the emphasis on the continuous care of the infant within the home by the mother as fundamentally oppressive to women. Margaret Mead, for instance, reacted swiftly to Bowlby's theory of maternal deprivation, calling it 'a new and subtle form of anti-feminism in which men – under the guise of exalting the importance of maternity – are tying women more tightly to their children than has been thought necessary since the invention of bottle feeding and baby carriages' (Mead, 1954).

Others, like Simone de Beauvoir, who perceived women's maternal function as the root of their oppression, saw the *idealization* of motherhood, which Bowlby helped to perpetuate, as problematic for women (de Beauvoir, 1953). For one thing, it diverted attention away from the reality of bringing up a child and led women to have unrealistic expectations of themselves as mothers. It also made it difficult for women to openly acknowledge – both to themselves and to others – their negative feelings about motherhood, which in turn helped to preserve the illusion of the ideal mother.

That some women did feel indifferent, frustrated, angry, guilty, at not 'simply' enjoying their infant, as the experts claimed they naturally would, became increasingly apparent in the early sixties. Betty Friedan, in her book *The Feminine Mystique* (1963), describes a growing discontent, primarily among white married, middle-class American women who, as housewives and mothers, felt isolated in the home. She speaks of the 'problem that has no name' which lay

> buried unspoken for many years in the minds of American women. It was a strange stirring, a sense of dissatisfaction, a yearning that women suffered in the middle of the twentieth century in the United States. Each suburban wife struggled with it alone. As she made the beds, shopped for groceries, matched slipcover material, ate peanut butter sandwiches with her children, chauffered Cub Scouts and Brownies, lay beside her husband at night, she was afraid to ask even of herself the silent question: 'Is this all?' (Friedan, 1963, p. 13)

In Britain Hannah Gavron's study *The Captive Wife: Conflicts of Housebound Mothers*, published in 1966, also highlighted the dissatisfaction of both working- and middle-class women in their role as housewives and mothers (although their dissatisfactions varied according to social class). What Friedan had called 'the problem that has no name' was beginning to acquire one. The 'captive wife' and the 'housebound mother' were about to emerge as a new social problem.

It was not only the way many women felt which challenged how motherhood was portrayed in the fifties. The steady increase in the number of married women with young children going out to work was in direct contradiction to the romantic view of motherhood and the family, which emphasized the importance of women staying at home to look after their children. This was reflected in the dissension which existed between some government departments at that time. The Ministry of Health, for example, emphasized the importance of women's role in the home as wives and mothers. The Ministry of Labour, on the other hand, wanted more married women to return to work. Women were needed as a 'reserve army of labour' to facilitate the rapid expansion of industries producing consumer goods, primarily for the home. Also, it was their wages, their 'pin-money', which would help to pay for these goods and sustain demand.

The challenge which women's employment posed to post-war theories of motherhood was at least partly resisted by the fact that women were working to buy goods which, the advertisers claimed, would help to make home life more enjoyable for all the family. Also, despite the fact that women's dual role was recognized, it was always understood that a woman's main duty was as wife and mother. For women the real-life difficulties of trying to manage conflicting role expectations and work demands were harder to avoid, and by the end of the fifties and the beginning of the sixties this was becoming more and more apparent. If the economy could no longer afford the idealized views of the childcare experts of the fifties, then neither could women.

Childrearing advice in the 1970s and 1980s

During the 1970s and 1980s there was a movement towards a more realistic, less idealized approach to motherhood. Increasingly childcare books acknowledged the work and the worry, as well as the pleasures and satisfactions, that having a child can bring. Women are told that if they do sometimes experience strong negative feelings towards their children they should not feel guilty, or that they are failing as a mother. Motherhood is not always fun, and women should not expect automatically to love their children. For example, in *Understanding Your Child From Birth To Three* Joseph Church states that

Most parents, determined to be loving come what may, do not antici-
pate the occasional rage they inevitably feel towards a baby who
demands so much. They then feel guilty, as though rage were their
own unique weakness. . . . Obviously parents have to control their
rage, but there is nothing abnormal about feeling it. (Church, 1976,
pp. 8–9)

This represents an important change from earlier advice. Similarly, the growing recognition that 'parents have needs too', suggests a move towards a more sympathetic and sensitive approach
to the mother.

There were also signs, by the mid-1970s, that experts were
beginning to question traditional family roles, in using terms such
as 'parent' or 'caretaker' rather than 'mother', even though the
majority of books addressed to 'parents' continued to assume that
the child's main caretaker would be the mother.

By the mid–1980s this trend was more pronounced. Most
authors of childrearing advice books encouraged fathers to
become more involved in the care of their children. (Although
underlying such advice very often was the assumption that fathers
would have to fit this in around paid employment.) Some books
even mentioned the possibility of parents reversing roles or sharing the care of their children equally. In *The Babycare Book*,
for example, Miriam Stoppard makes it clear that she believes
childrearing should be the joint responsibility of men and women
when she states that 'parenting and childrearing must be equally
shared' (Stoppard, 1984).

The development of an active feminist movement during the
late sixties and early seventies also helped publicise the view that
motherhood can be problematic. Although childcare experts and
feminists may agree on this, their analysis of the problems and
dissatisfaction women experience are likely to differ. Within feminist accounts women's experience as mothers is generally understood in relation to the way in which childcare is organized in
society: with women having major if not sole responsibility for
the care of children. Within contemporary childcare literature, in
contrast, a more common explanation for the dissatisfaction and
discontent women often experience as mothers is lack of self-
confidence. Having little or no direct experience in caring for
children, as is the case for many women nowadays, is frequently
cited as one of the reasons why women should feel lacking in self-

confidence. The possible uncertainty and confusion resulting from a diverse and ever-changing childcare literature is another.

There is an interesting contradiction here. On the one hand, experts have begun to acknowledge that their advice may lead to mothers feeling more self-conscious about their relationship with their children, and may undermine their self-confidence. Yet they nevertheless clearly believe that mothers still need them. One way in which this contradiction is partially avoided is by conceptualizing a different role for the expert. The newer emphasis is no longer on telling women what they should or should not do with their children, but on giving 'support' and 'guidance' where it is needed. The aim is to provide parents with a general knowledge of babies and small children, which they can then use in making their own decisions about what is best for their baby.

Linked in with this is the idea that because each child is different there can be no absolute rules to follow in childrearing, only guidelines. It is up to the person who has greatest knowledge and experience of the individual child – which, despite the wider usage of the term 'parent', is usually assumed to be the child's mother – to decide what would or would not be good for her.

The view of mothers as experts on their own children is within the tradition of childrearing advice in the 1950s, which stressed that mothers naturally knew best how to care for their children. Also, while the expectation on women to enjoy their infants may have been relaxed somewhat, it has not disappeared. Penelope Leach's *Baby and Child Care*, for example, is described in terms which are not dissimilar to what Martha Wolfenstein (1955) referred to as the 'fun morality' of the fifties.

> . . . this whole book is orientated towards you and your child as a unit of mutual pleasure-giving. Fun for him is fun for you. Fun for you creates more for him, and the more fun you all have the fewer will be your problems. (Leach, 1984, p. 21)

Similarly, although increasingly baby books acknowledge that what is good for the baby need not necessarily be good for the mother, we should be careful not to overestimate the extent to which this is about women's needs and not their children's. For example, Benjamin Spock in the revised edition of *Baby and Child Care* accepts with reserve mothers working, on the grounds that they may otherwise be unhappy. But the person whose happiness Spock is really concerned about is the child's.

A few mothers, particularly those with professional training, feel that they must work because they wouldn't be happy otherwise. I wouldn't disagree if a mother felt strongly about it, provided she had an ideal arrangement for her children's care. After all, an unhappy mother can't bring up very happy children. (Spock, 1973, p. 500)

Within the childcare literature of the 1970s and 1980s the assumption remains that babies need a lot of attention and that, by and large, it is mothers who will provide this. Previously it was to avoid any lasting emotional damage to the child that mothers were urged to give their full-time attention to their children. Whilst this is a view which is still widely held, there is now an additional pressure on women to stay at home and look after their children. They are also told that, lacking the one-to-one attention which they could give, their child might miss out on important learning experiences.

The focus of concern has shifted from emotional to intellectual development. Influenced by the theories of Jean Piaget, the emphasis is now on advising mothers on how to respond to their children in ways that will encourage intellectual growth. Apart from conversing with their infants, mothers are advised on ways in which a baby's mind can be stimulated by appropriate play and toys.

It is this assumption, that if we try we can make our babies cleverer, which creates the demand for 'educational toys' now found not only in toy shops, but also in places called 'Early Learning Centres'. Flash cards at the ready or not, one possible implication of this trend towards new standards of juvenile achievement is that increasingly it is the mother's fault if the baby does not learn.

A further trend within childcare literature is the shift towards providing more down-to-earth, practical advice for parents. Hugh Jolly's *Book of Child Care*, first published in 1975, is perhaps one of the best-known British books of this kind. Books like this have increasingly been thought to be necessary because of the trend towards smaller families, which means that few of us nowadays have much knowledge or experience of caring for a child prior to becoming a parent. Apart from the efforts of Hugh Jolly and others to provide practical information, it has also been suggested that courses in 'parentcraft' should be made available. One might compare such developments with the movement earlier this century to teach the essentials of mothercraft, especially to working-class women.

Although there has been some acknowledgement of the possible benefits that 'preparation for parenthood' would have for women, for example, helping them to feel less uncertain and anxious as mothers, the main concern has been about what effects such preparation could have on the next generation. In a now famous speech given in 1972, the then British secretary for social services, Sir Keith Joseph, raised the question of whether a policy of education for parenthood would help to break the 'cycles of deprivation' which, he suggested, underlay a number of important social and educational problems. (Pugh, 1980). Margaret Thatcher's government also made good political use of such ideas during the eighties, often reducing complex social problems to the level of poor childrearing practices. Seemingly it was parents and, to some extent, teachers who were at fault for all manner of social ills ranging from rising divorce figures to the growth in violent crime.

In the context of the present discussion of trends within childcare advice, these somewhat deterministic arguments for 'schools for mothers', and to a lesser extent fathers, are mainly of interest for the recognition they give to the learnt aspects of mothering. During the forties and fifties, as I have already outlined, experts played down the need for training in childcare. Instead the emphasis was on maternal instinct, defined as a natural desire to want to have and to care for children *and* an instinctive knowledge of what a child needs and how to provide it. The newer emphasis is to recognize the need for expert information and guidance, whilst maintaining a belief in maternal instinct as a set of feelings towards pregnancy and children which women have – or should have. For example, *The Baby Book*, presented free by some hospitals and clinics, states:

> Don't worry if you don't feel a great surge of maternal love all at once; it's all there just waiting to develop. Give yourself and your baby time to get to know each other.

It goes on:

Try to steer a happy middle course between letting your natural maternal instinct guide you without ignoring sensible advice from experienced people around you. (Morris, 1983, p. 45)

Despite these changes, some concepts which have become widely accepted within the literature over the last twenty years do not appear to have filtered through and become influential at a more general level. An example is the idea that the naturalness of maternal behaviour resides not in any specialised maternal instinct but in an ability which both women *and* men share.

Mothering as communication

By the seventies, psychological research into the relationship between mother and child had begun to take a new direction. There was a move away from Bowlby's attachment theory, towards a communicational analysis of mothering. This blossoming of an interest in the process of mothering, as distinct from the practice of childcare, owed a great deal to a redefinition of the child as active rather than passive in her own development. Previously it had been thought that a child was *made* social through the combined efforts of those involved in her upbringing. Most researchers, including Bowlby, now regarded this one-sided view of socialization as inaccurate. They suggested instead that the mother's relationship with her child was a two-way, interactive process, with mother influencing child and child influencing mother.

The relationship with the mother had previously been regarded as important because of its assumed significance for the later emotional development of the child. Lack of any substantive evidence to support this assumption assisted this shift of interest away from the long-term consequences of the child's relationship with its mother, towards a new emphasis on its more immediate effects.

If different questions were being asked about the mother–child relationship, different techniques were also being developed to study it. In these more recent studies it was not the infant's or the mother's behaviour being studied, but the way in which the one affected the other. Most typically, studies used slowed-down video recordings of infants responding to their mothers, and vice-versa, as a way of finding out about how mother and child interact. Such detailed examination revealed that infants can and do affect the way in which their mothers respond to them. We also know that infants are, even at birth, capable of selectively attending to the world around them. The fact that it is people whom babies find most interesting to listen to and look at ensures that they receive our attention. Quite simply, if a baby stares into our eyes we will most likely assume she is looking meaningfully at us and respond with looks, smiles or baby talk.

What was being suggested is that mothers, or indeed any human being, will readily interpret what an infant does *as if* it were meant to communicate something. However, for mothers to feel that babies have wishes, intentions and feelings which can be communicated to others, they first need to be able to identify in their infant's gestures and vocalizations patterns of behaviour which are familiar to them as ways of saying something. They need, in other words, to be able to recognize and label what it is that their infant is doing (was that a yawn/a frown/a gurgle?) before they can interpret her actions (she's sleepy/she's uncomfortable/she wants a love), which in turn will guide their own responses (I'd better put her to bed/change her nappy/give her a cuddle).

Much of the research into the nature of mother-child interactions has tried to demonstrate that infant behaviour is organized in such a way that it will seem meaningful to other human beings. Colwyn Trevarthen, for example, claimed that an infant's gestures and vocalisations are not random, but are finely timed sequences of behaviour. It is this periodicity, he argued, which gives much of what the infant does the appearance of an attempt to communicate and enables us to begin communicating with babies, probably right from the moment they are born (Trevarthen, 1979).

Studies in the 1970s attempted to describe in detail the exact nature of these early communications or dialogues, in particular those between mother and child. What these studies showed was that the behaviour of infant and mother is a finely synchronized exchange, with mother and infant taking it in turns to 'say' something. Kenneth Kaye, for instance, described how with both breast- and bottle-feeding mothers there seemed to be a dialogue-like exchange going on during feeding. He found that, generally speaking, mothers did not interrupt their infants whilst they were feeding, but tended instead to interact with them more during the periods when they paused from sucking (Kaye, 1977).

The analogy which Daniel Stern used is of a dance, where both partners know the steps and the music by heart and can therefore move precisely together (Stern, 1977). Mothers and infants are not, however, equally versed in the art of 'dance'. Studies have shown that what may appear to be a smooth interchange taking place between mother and baby is, at first, the result of the mother modifying her behaviour to fit in with what her infant is doing. It is the mother, in other words, who is responsible for producing the highly synchronized patterns of interaction which Kaye and others observed. Gradually, as infants learn the skills of turn-taking and also come to understand the modifying effects of their own and other people's behaviour, true dialogues, which are two-sided, become possible. This is usually not until the infant reaches the end of her first year (Schaffer, 1977b).

This communicational analysis of the mother–child relationship has potentially important implications for notions of maternal responsibility and blame. Once again, it would seem that mothers have new, ever more complex duties which they are expected to perform for their children. They are seen as responsible not only for a child's emotional development, as in the 1950s, but also for facilitating the development of shared meanings and communicative skills, which are necessary for the child to become a humanly responsive member of the society into which she is born.

To do this successfully it is claimed that mothers need to credit their infant with having thoughts, feelings and intentions similar to other human beings. They also need to modify their own behaviour to fit in with what their infant is doing. Sensitive or good mothering is, in this sense, a skill, the skill of responding to a particular infant in a reciprocal and synchronised manner. According to Schaffer this ought not to be too difficult:

> She (the mother) rarely does anything without being aware of her child's precise requirements or without adapting her behaviour in their light. The younger the child the greater her need to adapt in this way, and it is one of the wonders of nature that mothers (or almost any adult confronted by a small baby) can make these changes so naturally and spontaneously that they may not even be fully aware of what they are doing. (Schaffer, 1977a, p. 84)

Despite the existence of important differences from the views of the experts of the forties and fifties, there are echoes of earlier permissive approaches in Schaffer's remarks. For example, his suggestion that mothering is, by and large, a natural, unconscious process might well be subscribed to by Bowlby or Winnicott. Also, in emphasizing the importance of the mother organizing her behaviour around what the infant is doing, interactive studies to some extent continued in the child-centred tradition of the forties and fifties. Once again there is an acceptance on the part of the experts that it is vital for the child's social, intellectual and emotional development that the mother adapts herself to her infant's rather than her own needs. Previously, definitions of women's needs – largely in terms of a desire to make their infants happy – allowed experts to claim that this was something which women did naturally and easily. For Schaffer, allowing oneself to be 'phased' by one's infant is also regarded as unproblematic. It is 'one of the wonders of nature', something most mothers do 'naturally and spontaneously' whenever they are with their infants.

As with earlier permissive childrearing advice, there is also a lack of attention to real-life problems, such as poverty and the emotional stresses women may experience in childrearing, in this more recent approach to understanding the mother and child. As Denise Riley remarks: 'It speaks only of the activities of a time-less, ahistorical, desert island mother-child couple, watched at its communications and interactions as in a bell-jar' (Riley, 1983a, p. 20).

Despite these apparent similarities, a communicational analysis of mothering differs markedly from earlier approaches in what it defines as natural about mothering. In contrast to traditional beliefs about motherhood, it suggests that the naturalness of 'maternal' behaviour resides not in any special maternal intuition or instinct, but in the ability which all human beings share of being able to respond to babies, right from birth, as if they were already human beings. Beyond this it is claimed that mothering is a learned skill which develops through learning and experience with individual children. Rather than anything in women's (or men's) nature, it is the social conditions, which shape our indi-vidual motivations and opportunities to interact with infants, which will primarily determine whether or not we make good mothers. On this basis there ought to be no reason why men should not make good 'mothers', providing they are willing and able to spend the necessary time and effort.

Can men be mothers?

Theories of the child and mother which emerged in the 1970s and 1980s have potentially radical implications for the way motherhood is traditionally defined: as a role that is naturally best suited to and best carried out by women. Such implications have, to some extent, been recognised from the beginning. For example, in the conclusion to his book *Mothering* Schaffer repeatedly emphasises the point that 'mother can be male':

> Mother need not be the biological mother: *she can be any person of either sex* [sic] . . . There is, for that matter, no reason why the mothering role should not filled as competently by males as females. . . . Thus all the original reasons for confining childcare to women are disappearing: *mother need not be a woman!* . . . from the child's point of view it matters little what sex mother is. (Schaffer, 1977a, pp. 111–2)

Unfortunately Schaffer's choice of words belies what he is saying. Not only does he use the term mother to describe the person who is primarily responsible for the care of the child, but he reaffirms its traditionally gender-specific meaning by constantly referring to mother as she.

Schaffer does extend the possibility of mothering to adults who are not necessarily the child's biological parents. This not only has implications for how we regard men's involvement in childcare, but also for the increasing number of women caring for children to whom they are biologically unrelated. For example, women who are responsible for the care of their male partner's children from a previous marriage.

We should be careful, however, to distinguish arguments for men's greater involvement in childcare based on the assumption that there is no essential difference in the ability of women and men to care for a child, and the increasing interest in fathers and fatherhood. A relatively ignored area until the 1980s, there now exists a rapidly growing literature on fatherhood. Much of the research tends to fall into three main categories: the influence of men on a child's development (for example, Lamb, 1981); men's experience of fatherhood (for example, Beail and McGuire, 1982; McKee and O'Brien, 1982); and father's participation in childcare and the constraints on this (for example, Lewis & O'Brien, 1987; Russell, 1983). Others have studied the recent interest in father-hood itself, and have asked why fathers have become a popular research topic. Does it reflect men's greater responsibility and involvement in childcare, or is it an attempt by men to reaffirm their power within the family (Pollock and Sutton, 1987)?

Whilst it may pose a challenge to traditional beliefs about what fathers can and do contribute to the care of their children, by focusing on the specific contribution fathers can make, a good deal of the work on fatherhood lends support to the view that women and men have different, albeit equally important, parts to play in a child's upbringing. This particularly applies to studies that are concerned with how fathers, as men, influence their children's development.

The debate over whether there is an essential similarity or an essential difference between women and men, in their ability to care for children, is also present in feminist writing and thinking. The former viewpoint can be found in those strands of feminism which emphasize that gender equality is dependent on women and men having equal share in, and equal responsibility for, all aspects of childcare, thereby enabling women to participate equally with men in paid work outside the home. A communicational analysis of motherhood is potentially supportive of such a perspective, in so far as it acknowledges that there is no reason why the person who has major responsibility for the care of an infant should be a woman or, for that matter, biologically related. The recent emphasis on the importance of fatherhood as a distinct male role, on the other hand, is not necessarily supportive. Although it may appear to provide evidence for the view that men should have a greater involvement in childcare, it is basically unsupportive because of its fundamental acceptance of different and distinct roles for women and men within the family.

The belief that women and men have essentially different contri-butions to make in childrearing was an important aspect of femin-ist thinking during the early part of this century. The Swedish feminist Ellen Key, for example, argued that because of natural biological differences between the sexes women were better able than men to care for children. Such arguments were seen as benefiting women, given the positive role and elevated status accorded motherhood and the relatively few alternatives available to women during that period. To say that men were biologically unsuitable for such a role would, in that context, have had a certain appeal for many women.

The form that feminism took in the inter-war period and the years after the Second World War continued along this line of thinking (Banks, 1981). It was not until the late sixties, with the emergence of the women's liberation movement, that feminists seriously began to oppose the assumption that women, and not men, should be the primary carers of children. Feminists also asked how a belief in maternal instinct constrains women's lives. The following chapter examines this and other possible influences on why women do or do not have children.

4

Reproduction: a woman's right to choose?

Why are some women mothers and others not? The usual way of tackling this question is to suggest possible reasons why a woman does not have any children. She's not married. She's infertile. She's not interested. But we might just as well ask, why do so many women become mothers?

This is a question which, until relatively recently, has rarely been written about.or discussed; a predictable position, when one considers that for most of this century motherhood has been defined as the natural outcome of an inborn, instinctual desire in women for maternity. To ask, 'Why do women have children?' is not merely novel, it is to 'start a revolution in the way that we think about women and about motherhood' (Dowrick and Grundberg, 1980). It is to imply that there is some choice in the matter.

Choice is not a very meaningful word unless it is used in relation to the circumstances in which people live their lives. Women are not all equally able to choose to have – or not to have – children. The lesbian who sees having children as impractical, if not impossible, and who has taken in society's view that having a child would be wrong and bad for the child: can she be said to have made a choice not to have children? Or, alternatively, consider the working-class woman who can foresee no other future for herself besides being on the dole or working in a dead-end job for very little money. To what extent can her decision to get married and have children be usefully regarded as a choice?

I am not, of course, suggesting that these are the only possible options available to lesbians and working-class women, nor that such 'decisions' cannot ever be experienced as a real and positive choice by the women making them. I am merely illustrating that choice is a highly complex and possibly deceptive word to use to describe women's potential to have – or not to have – children. Clearly we must acknowledge the limitations to choice for women in both of these respects. We must ask what are the major constraints and permissions, both social and psychological, which enable and compel women either to become mothers or, in far fewer cases, to decide not to have children.

The choice not to have children

An increasing number of women are choosing not to have children. For some this is because they do not like children, or perhaps they think they would not make very good mothers. They may want to devote most of their time and energy to a career, and feel it would be difficult or even wrong to try to combine a career with motherhood. Others may be motivated by a concern with overpopulation, or believe that with high rates of unemployment, poverty and the threat of nuclear war, the world is not a fit place into which to bring a child. Other women may feel that unless they could provide the 'very best' for a child, both materially and emotionally, they would not want to have one. This may include having a close and apparently permanent relationship with someone else. There are also many women who just do not want children. They may like children, but not the idea of having any themselves. Whatever their reasons, how able are women to exercise this choice if they do decide they do not want children?

Throughout all our lives we are bombarded with do's and don'ts which reinforce expectations in ourselves and others about the sort of women we should be. These expectations function as social pressures and reduce the opportunity to make genuine choices about the way we may want to live our lives. Such pressures are most acute in connection with reproduction and sexuality. Women are expected to desire both men and motherhood. Indeed, as women we are socialized to believe that having children is nice, natural and necessary. Not to have children (and, similarly, not to have relationships with men) can therefore be a difficult choice to make. It means going against all the social pressures which inform women they ought to become mothers.

Such pressures operate on women to varying degrees. Some women are encouraged and allowed to have children, whilst others are not. This illustrates an important contradiction in social beliefs about motherhood. In addition to the belief that all women have a strong desire for maternity, there also exists the view that only women in stable heterosexual relationships should be encouraged to have children. For this reason, it is married women who are likely to experience greatest difficulty in exercising the choice not to have children – let alone perceiving they have a choice. Selfish, immature, irresponsible, unnatural, inadequate: these are just some of the words which may be used to describe women who choose a childless or, more positively, child-free marriage. Similarly, married women seeking an abortion may meet with resistance from doctors who regard them as pathological or just plain wrong in their decision (Macintyre, 1976; Boyle, 1992). The married woman who does not want children will have to be determined if she is going to achieve her aim, and not give way to the pressures on her to change her mind. This can be hard without support for one's decision. Apart from friends and family, who very often are a major source of pressure to have children, society affords married women very little support in this respect.

The feminist movement, in demanding that women should have 'the right to choose' how to live their lives, has actively defended the right of individual women to decide when and if to have children. Further support for the decision not to have children is provided by organizations concerned with population growth. In a world already stretched in terms of resources by overpopulation, not having children can be seen as a socially responsible thing to do. However, although such arguments may provide further validation for the choice not to have children, the fundamental concern of ecological movements is not the protection of women's rights but of world resources.

Control over reproduction: contraception

Apart from the social pressures – on married, heterosexual women especially – to become mothers, women's ability to choose to remain child-free will also depend on whether they are able to prevent or terminate an unwanted pregnancy. It is a popular misconception that because modern methods of birth control are highly reliable women are relatively free to choose whether or not to have a child. This is both oversimplified and, very often, inaccurate. Not every baby born is the result of a planned pregnancy, nor is the ability to control fertility accessible to all women. Many women lack knowledge of how to get and use contraception, though knowledge about contraceptives and how to obtain them does not guarantee control over their use. Certainly with the more effective forms of contraception it is the medical profession and the drug industry who control access to information and services. For instance, if a woman wants to go on the pill or, alternatively, use an intra-uterine device (IUD), diaphragm or cervical cap, she cannot do so without first obtaining the permission of a doctor or clinic.

The Gillick case was an example of legal control over the use of contraception. In December 1984 the English courts ruled in agreement with Mrs Victoria Gillick, a Catholic mother of ten, that it was illegal for doctors to give contraceptive advice or treatment to persons under the age of sixteen without their parents' consent, save in cases of 'emergency'. What constitutes an emergency is an interesting question. If a fifteen-year-old girl is engaging in unprotected intercourse and is at risk of an unplanned pregnancy, as well as the possibility of infection with HIV or other sexually transmitted diseases, perhaps it could be considered an emergency to give her advice on contraception and disease prevention. The court's decision was later reversed. Had it not been, girls would have been denied the right to make important decisions about reproduction and sexuality for themselves.

This is not to say that girls always have access to sex education and resources to understand sexuality and control their fertility. Getting sympathetic and informed advice about how to use contraceptives continues to be a problem for many young women. In Britain, cuts in the National Health Service have resulted in the closure of many family planning clinics. There has also been slow progress in developing, on a widespread scale, sex education in schools, which provides opportunities for discussing attitudes towards contraception and abortion, as well as giving detailed information. Unfortunately, there seems little reason to expect any substantial improvement in educational standards as a result of the 1988 Education (No. 2) Act, which gives parents the right to decide whether their child receives sex education in school and governors the right to decide what that education should be.

Even if women have access to contraceptives and know how to use them, they may be prevented from using an efficient method of birth control because it would conflict with their religious beliefs or those of their partners. The Catholic church in particular has not shifted from its position of disapproving of all methods of birth control other than those deemed to be 'natural'. Even in the face of AIDS, it remains generally opposed to the use of condoms, whether for disease prevention or birth control. Others may find certain contraceptive methods unacceptable, despite their high reliability, because they may involve a risk to themselves. For example, the intra-uterine device (IUD) or coil works well for some women but it can pose health risks (the Dalkon Shield is an IUD which has now been withdrawn from use because it caused major complications and deaths in women all over the world). It may cause heavier periods and bleeding, increase the risk of pelvic and uterine infection, as well as occasionally perforating the uterus or cervix. If it fails as a contraceptive device it can cause complications, including miscarriage.

Among the side-effects and health risks associated with taking the pill are nausea, headaches, weight gain, bleeding between periods, water retention, depression, sore breasts and an increased susceptibility to some vaginal infections. More serious side-effects include high blood pressure, possibly cancer and, more rarely, liver problems and thrombosis. There is also an increased risk of heart disease, especially in women who smoke and/or are over thirty-five.

Banned as a general contraceptive method in the United States, Depo Provera has been shown to cause breast and uterine cancer in animals. Depo Provera is not a pill, but a contraceptive injection given every three months. The advantage to this is that, unlike the pill which a woman has to remember to take every day, once the injection has been given a woman does not have to think about contraception again for some time. This and the fact that it can be administered to large numbers of women quickly and simply makes it ideally suited for population control, which is how it has been used in the Third World. Quite rightly, this has led to accusations that Depo Provera is being used in a racist way (Rakusen, 1981). Certainly, both the manufacturers – the American company Upjohn – and international family planning agencies have put pressure on developing nations to use the drug. The commonest side-effect in Depo Provera's use is unpredictable bleeding. Many women have heavy, prolonged bleeding or persistent spotting; others do not bleed at all. Other side-effects can include nausea, cramps, headaches, weight gain and backache. Sometimes the side-effects continue long after the three month period of contraceptive effectiveness, and infertility may also be prolonged for some time after a woman has stopped using Depo Provera. There may also be more serious health risks associated with long-term use, for example an increased risk of cervical cancer.

Apart from the health risks, it can also be argued that Depo Provera places control over fertility even more firmly in the hands of the medical profession and those who have a vested interest in population control, most especially multi-national drug companies. This is certainly the view taken by many Western and Third World feminist groups and organisations, who have actively campaigned for an end to the use of Depo Provera.

In Britain Depo Provera was approved for long-term use following a public inquiry in 1984. This reversed a decision, made by the government two years earlier, to refuse to license Depo Provera for long-term use because it was considered that the risks were too great. Many women have since been prescribed the drug. Concerns have been expressed that Black women in particular may be pressurized into accepting Depo Provera (or sterilization) following an abortion, and that injectable contraceptives are often administered to women with learning difficulties who may not be able to give 'informed consent'. Practices of this kind raise important questions about abuses in reproductive health care and women's lack of control.

Such concerns were further reinforced, in 1987, by the sterilization case of a seventeen-year-old woman with severe learning difficulties. The House of Lords' decision was that the courts can authorize a sterilization operation in such cases, where it is necessary to ensure 'for a woman's own safety and welfare that she does not become pregnant'. In another case that year a high court judge ruled that a doctor could carry out an abortion on a 25-year-old woman with learning difficulties without her consent.

This case is notable as it is the first time such a decision appears to have been for an adult.

The use of the courts' powers to 'protect' women in this way is opposed by those who feel that with better information on contraception and sexuality for women and men alike, the question of sterilization need not necessarily arise. Interestingly, the sterilization argument has not been suggested in relation to men.

The attitudes women have about their bodies, and about sex, will also be important in the contraceptive choices they each feel able to make. The pill is not only highly reliable and easy to use, but it is also non-intrusive. These are some of the reasons why, despite the various side-effects and health risks associated with its use, the pill is still recommended to, and taken by, many women. Condoms have no health risks and when used consistently and correctly, in conjunction with a spermicide, they are a very effective method of birth control. They also reduce the risk of cervical cancer and sexually transmitted infections like HIV (the virus which causes AIDS). Their one major disadvantage is that a woman has to rely on a man being willing to wear one.

The diaphragm or cap is a female-controlled contraceptive. It too has few side-effects or health risks, and is very reliable if used properly with a spermicide. Like the condom, it may also help to protect against sexually transmitted diseases and reduce the risk of cervical cancer. However some women dislike putting their fingers in their vagina; for others putting in a cap in 'readiness' for intercourse may seem either too embarrassing or too calculating an approach to sex to enable them to use one.

The sponge is a female contraceptive which is non-intrusive and has few side-effects. It has the added advantage that it does not require medical intervention. Introduced into Britain in 1985, the sponge is the first modern contraceptive method available to be used by women which can be obtained over the counter without a prescription. Unfortunately on its own it is not a reliable method of birth control and should only be used as a back up for other methods, such as the condom.

Another method of birth control which offers women the opportunity of controlling their own fertility without the need for medical involvement, which is both safe and potentially reliable, is fertility awareness. Based on the Billings method developed some years ago (Billings *et al.*, 1974), this method teaches women to recognize the changes in their own bodies which each month signal fertility, for instance changes in body temperature and cervical mucus. They can then plan their sex lives accordingly, if they wish to avoid becoming pregnant, or need use contraception only during their fertile period when unprotected intercourse would be risky. It has been claimed that if it is used properly this method can be as much as 97 per cent effective (Drake and Drake, 1984). However it takes time to learn fertility awareness and feel confident with it; it also requires the co-operation of men.

Helen Roberts has documented the pervasiveness of male control in family planning as it operates through the church, the state, the medical profession, drug companies and the structure of women's relationships with men (Roberts, 1981). Both the degree of control women have within a relationship and the sexual attitudes of their male partners will seriously affect the contraceptive choices women feel able to make.

As part of the social construction of male sexuality many men come to believe that sex is more important and more uncontrollable for them than it is for women; that men and not women should take the sexual initiative; and that what counts as 'having sex' is penetration of the vagina by the penis, preferably without a condom. Such beliefs limit the control women have over both sexuality and reproduction. For instance, women who have sex with men who insist on intercourse are being denied the opportunity of controlling their fertility through the safe, very reliable method of engaging in non-penetrative sex. In other situations it may be men's resistance to using condoms, or indeed any form of contraception, which is the issue. How can we talk about choice when many women are afraid, often for very good reasons, to say no to men who want to engage in unprotected intercourse? When we talk about reproductive rights we are not simply talking about better health service delivery or sex education; we are also talking about the role heterosexuality plays in the oppression of women.

Abortion

As long as there is no contraceptive which is 100 per cent safe and effective, access to safe, legal, free abortion on demand is essential if women are to be able to choose whether or not to become mothers. The important role that abortion plays in fertility control is demonstrated by the frequency of its use. In 1990, 171 500 legal abortions were carried out in England and Wales.

Prior to 1967 relatively few women could obtain a legal abortion in Britain. However years of campaigning by the Abortion Law Reform Association led, finally, to the passing of the 1967 Abortion Act. Though it undoubtedly widened the grounds for abortion, by introducing the possibility of social as well as medical reasons for a lawful termination, this Act by no means made abortion legal. What it did was to make abortion no longer a crime under certain circumstances. They are: when it is carried out before 24 weeks of pregnancy, with the certification of two doctors to the effect that either, the pregnancy is likely to end in the birth of a handicapped child or, is a danger to the health of the mother or any existing child of hers. One further criteria is that any danger in continuing with the pregnancy must be considered by the doctors to be greater than the dangers involved in ending it.

Abortion is not available to all women equally, nor is it a woman's right in terms of being freely available on demand. A woman's chances of getting an abortion will depend on the attitude of her doctor, on whether the doctor decides that hers is a lawful and deserving case. That many doctors will not or cannot, due to long waiting lists, agree to a woman's request for an abortion is reflected in the massive numbers of women who are forced to pay to have a private abortion. Just over half the abortions carried out in 1990 in England and Wales were done privately.

Cuts in National Health Service facilities are likely to constrain choice even further, forcing more and more women – those who can afford to pay – to turn to the private sector, making what should be a right a luxury for many women. Denying public funds for abortion has greatest impact on the reproductive freedom of poor women, since they are least able to afford abortions. The average cost of an abortion is between £250 and £300, a great deal of money to the young, the poor and the unemployed. The implications of this are clearly worrying. Denied access to legal, safe, free or low-cost abortion women may turn to a back-street abortionist or attempt to abort themselves. Alternatively, they may feel they have no option but to have the child.

Apart from the legal and medical control over women's access to abortion, women's choices are also affected by what they have come to know, and feel, about abortion. The church plays a powerful role in this respect via its teachings on abortion as morally wrong. Debates have raged for centuries about the moral acceptability of abortion. More recently, this debate has been between pro-choice and anti-abortion groups. Those who are pro-choice argue that abortion should be free and available to every woman on demand, on the grounds that women should have the right to decide whether or not to have a child. Others, such as the so-called 'pro-life' organizations, Life and The Society for the Protection of the Unborn Child, oppose abortion on the grounds that from the moment of fertilization the embryo, and later the foetus, is an unborn child with a 'right-to-life'. They want to make abortion illegal or, at the very least, more difficult to get than it already is.

There have been a number of unsuccessful attempts by anti-abortionists to change the law on abortion in Britain. In 1988 David Alton's Abortion Amendment Bill sought to reduce the time limit for abortion from 28 to 18 weeks. The argument given was that because of medical progress foetuses can now survive at an earlier stage (24 weeks). If it had succeeded this attack on women's rights would have particularly affected women who did not know they were pregnant, or were too scared to tell anyone, until late on in the pregnancy. It would also have meant that many women would no longer be able to decide to terminate a pregnancy on the grounds of foetal abnormality. At present, most foetal abnormalities can only be reliably diagnosed by tests which cannot be done until after 18 weeks.

The Bill would also have affected women seeking abortions in Britain because abortion is illegal or difficult to get in their own country. Many late abortions are carried out on women from Ireland, for instance, where abortion is illegal.

Although it was specifically aimed at preventing late terminations the Alton Bill was, in effect, anti-abortion. An alternative way of reducing the number of late abortions is by supporting women's rights to free abortion on demand. Delays within the National Health Service often result in women having abortions after 18 weeks, and the moral and legal circumstances surrounding abortion often make women feel afraid to seek advice until late in their pregnancies.

Although the Alton Bill was defeated, continued lobbying by anti-abortionists contributed to the British government's decision, two years later, to incorporate an abortion clause in the Human Fertilisation and Embryology Bill. The inclusion of an abortion clause to a Bill largely concerned with embryo research was seen as a victory for pro-Life (anti-choice) supporters, who argued, along the lines of the previous Powell Bill (p. 101), that it was ridiculous to provide embryos with legal protection after 14 days when abortion was permitted until 24 weeks. However, such a position denies the profound differences between abortion, involving a foetus in a woman's uterus, and embryo research, involving cells in a test tube. They are two kinds of procedures carried out for quite different purposes. On these grounds it was argued by Mary Warnock, who chaired the Committee of Inquiry into Human Fertilisation (Warnock Report, 1984), and others, including many feminists, that the issues of abortion and embryo research should be kept separate.

The Bill represented the first full test of parliamentary opinion on the issue of abortion since 1967, when David Steel's Abortion Amendment Act was passed. Surprisingly, given the apparent earlier success of the anti-abortionist lobby, far from tightening the law the outcome was a liberalising of the 1967 Act. Although MPs voted to reduce the time limit for legal abortion from 28 to 24 weeks, since doctors have not in practice been carrying out abortions after 24 weeks the change will make little difference to the number of terminations carried out (the number of late abortions carried out on the National Health Service was only 23 in 1988). The Commons went on to liberalize the law by removing any time limit to abortions needed to 'prevent grave permanent injury to the physical or mental health of the pregnant woman' or if there was 'substantial risk that if the child were born it would suffer such physical or mental abnormalities as to be seriously handicapped'. Previously this had stood at 28 weeks.

Anti-abortionists have had rather more success in restricting access to legal abortion in certain parts of the United States and in Canada. For example, in Quebec a High Court ruling, in 1989, upheld the view that a foetus is a human entity with a right to life and entitled to legal protection. This case also set a precedent in asserting the rights of men over the rights of women to have an abortion. The court upheld an injunction sought by the woman's

former boyfriend to prevent her from having an abortion, threatening her with a fine of $50,000 or two years in jail if she did not comply. This injunction was subsequently overturned by the Supreme Court of Canada, the same day as the woman, Chantal Daigle, had an abortion. In Britain there have been similar attempts by would-be fathers to stop women from having abortions. Although these have, so far, been unsuccessful, the Quebec case is an example of how strengthening the rights of fathers may negate the rights of women, in this case to abortion.

Other options?

The freedom to choose not to have children depends not only on a woman's control over her own fertility, but also on the options available to her for achieving a meaningful life. It involves having something else that you can and want to do with your life, other than becoming a mother. Unfortunately, for many young, Black and working-class women, due to the effects of gender, class and racial inequalities, the answer to the question 'What else could I do with my life?' is often a depressingly restricted one. Low paid work or living on welfare benefits may often seem to be the main alternatives. Is it surprising if women in these circumstances come to feel that having children is a more positive way of creating a sense of purpose and importance in their lives? This is especially so when one considers the romantic and idealized images of motherhood frequently presented to girls who, very often, have little or no experience of caring for young children with which they can compare. Several studies suggest that young women's expectations of motherhood, although often positive, reflect an awareness that opportunities are otherwise limited. They see motherhood as offering them a status and sense of power and control that they would not necessarily achieve through paid work (Sharpe, 1976; Griffin, 1986).

Women who manage to gain well-paid jobs with promotional prospects are obviously in a very different position. Given that it is still widely believed that a woman cannot be a proper mother and still carry on with a full-time job, the question of choice for women in these circumstances is often perceived as either children or a career. Some women decide not to have children because

they feel that to give up all they have worked for, and their independence, would be detrimental both to them and a child. They may also feel that combining paid employment and motherhood would be too demanding in terms of their time and energy, as well as having negative consequences for their career. Rarely do women reach the salary levels they might have expected had they not had children; and women who leave employment, even for a brief period, to have a child may find themselves out of the running for promotion when they return. One can hardly call this a real choice. It is a choice that is constrained by the fact that, given the way in which childcare and work are organized within society, paid employment and motherhood are often difficult roles to combine successfully and are generally regarded as alternatives.

So far I have talked about some of the constraints operating on a woman's choice not to have children. However, there is another side to the coin where reproductive rights are concerned, and that is whether all women who want children can have them. This is something which is discussed later in this and the following chapter on the new reproductive technologies, which makes clear that it is not only the involuntarily infertile who may benefit from such developments: lesbians, celibate and single heterosexual women may also have their choices widened. That this is rarely acknowledged says something very important about beliefs about who should – or should not – become mothers. It is this aspect of social control that I next want to consider.

The choice for children

What does having a child mean? This is an important question to ask if we are to understand how and why women come to desire maternity.

One answer is that having a child is seen as signifying development to a new, more adult, more mature stage of life. This is true for both women and men, though the pressures on women are far greater. Women are expected to regard motherhood as their most important adult role in life. One of the attractions of motherhood, therefore, is its normative quality. To become pregnant is to do what is expected of you. It is to be 'in the club' in more ways than one. It is to be the same as other women, to be 'one

of the girls' and enter into female friendship based on shared expectation and experience. Having children also brings status; it is the principal way in which a woman 'becomes socially recognised as being a "real" woman, a woman who has fulfilled her "true" destiny and role in life' (Gittins, 1985). Ann Phoenix's research with young mothers supports this view (Phoenix, 1991). She shows how the desire for motherhood is very much connected with the recognition of an apparent privilege denied to childless women.

Fathering a child can be seen as proving a man's virility, a concept that is central to definitions of masculinity, but a man retains his status even if he is childless. For women the connection between maternity and femininity is less specifically related to the assumption that people have babies because they have had sex. What is supposedly indicated in their case is the existence of a maternal instinct and a nurturing, caring personality – essential aspects of society's construction of what is both female and feminine.

The social pressures on women to be feminine are not easily put aside, particularly when the alternatives are made to seem unattractive or abnormal. Even if these pressures are resisted, there are other beliefs which may motivate women to want children. There is the belief, for example, that life with children is more emotionally satisfying and interesting than life without them. Whether this is true or not, children are often seen as providing us with an insurance policy against a lonely old age and, also, with a way of reliving our lives and our childhood. Apart from the vicarious satisfaction which this may bring, the feeling that our activities are beneficial to our children can also help to give purpose and meaning to what we do. The belief that having children is one way of ensuring some sort of immortality, either for ourselves or the family name, may also be important to some, particularly in an increasingly secular society.

Children are also believed to give purpose and stability to our selves and to heterosexual relationships. It is expected that married couples will 'naturally' want children. This being the case, motherhood may not be perceived as a choice by some married women, but almost as an inevitability. As one woman told me: 'It was something I just did. There was no choice'. Similarly, how

many non-biological mothers feel they have a choice? As women, it is expected they will look after their male partner's children.

Strong social pressures exist to ensure that women do come to regard motherhood as a necessary and desirable outcome of being married. This is clearly evident in attitudes towards married couples who do not have children. If a couple is childless by choice, control is likely to be exerted by defining them as selfish and irresponsible, but more especially the woman. 'After all, having children is what marriage is for!' Married women, if they do become pregnant, are not expected to want an abortion or give the baby up for adoption. If childlessness is the result of infertility then the form of control is likely to be different. In this case the notion that marriage entails having children is upheld by defining this as a problem that deserves our deepest sympathy and support.

In addition to the expectation that women who are married will want children, it is also still regarded as desirable that women who want children will marry. Such an assumption is evident in the negative way in which being pregnant and single has in the past generally been seen as a problem, despite the fact that many women choose to have children outside marriage and without men being involved in their upbringing.

Motherhood is generally regarded as an essential aspect of being female, the outcome of an instinctual force which, in varying amounts, all women are supposed to possess. How is it, then, that outside marriage a woman's desire to have children is questioned? As Sally Macintyre remarks: 'At its crudest, this leads to the position that the maternal instinct only operates in married women and not in unmarried women' (Macintyre, 1976, p. 159).

This potential contradiction in theories of motherhood has partly been avoided by invoking different explanations for why married and unmarried women want children. In the former case the usual explanation, if it can be usefully termed that, is that married women 'naturally' want to have babies; when a woman is not married other reasons are deemed necessary. In the past these have tended to be negative; for example, one way of accounting for a single woman wanting a child is to see this as the result of her needing to be needed and valued. Alternatively, it may be assumed that she has become pregnant as a way of trying to ensure that her partner will not leave her for someone else. In

both of these examples the assumption is that an unmarried woman becomes pregnant not because she really wants a child, but because motherhood appears to offer her a way in which she can satisfy other needs in her life. The implication is that single women (and lesbians) desire children for selfish/bad reasons. Married women 'are accorded a monopoly on acceptable reasons for wanting a child' (Radford, 1991).

Slightly more sympathetic accounts are those which regard pregnancy in women who are not married as accidental: the unfortunate outcome of contraceptive ignorance or carelessness or, less patronisingly, of contraceptive inefficiency. This view of the single mother as victim – of men, ignorance, misfortune, her own maternal instincts – has important social implications. In attributing pregnancy to forces beyond her conscious control a woman can be absolved responsibility for her actions, and if she 'can't help it' then, arguably, she ought not to be blamed or discriminated against.

This is an argument for tolerance, not approval. It is also an argument which ignores the fact that many women do not see why they should not have children just because they are not married or having a relationship with a man. An important social trend in the 1980s was the marked rise in the proportion of babies born in Britain outside marriage: from 12 per cent of all births in 1980 to 25 per cent in 1988 (FPSC, 1990). There are similar trends in the United States and parts of Europe: for example, in Sweden and Denmark it has been common for many years for unmarried couples to have children. Whatever their reasons, more and more women are having children outside marriage, and many are bringing them up independently. In Britain one in four children are now born to women who are not married, just over half of whom are living with a man. The other half includes lesbians, celibate and single heterosexual women. However it is lesbian mothers in particular who face the greatest opposition to women openly choosing to have children outside marriage.

The right to motherhood: lesbian mothers

Lesbians do not form a single group with the same experiences and needs, and becoming a mother will affect them in different ways. Nevertheless, lesbians will have certain shared experiences when it comes to having children, in particular society's definition of lesbian motherhood as either impossible or wrong.

The belief that lesbian motherhood is a contradiction in terms stems partly from the assumption that being a lesbian, a 'real lesbian' that is, means having sexual relationships with women and not men. Since vaginal intercourse is generally regarded as necessary for a woman to become pregnant, this leads to the conclusion that lesbians do not become mothers.

In fact, as various studies have demonstrated, there is no necessary association between identifying as a lesbian and only having sexual relationships with women. Nevertheless, many women do choose to have sexual relationships only with women and, in this case, it is the assumption that there is no possibility of their ever becoming pregnant which needs questioning.

It is sperm which is necessary for fertilization, not its ejaculation from a penis inserted into a woman's vagina. Nowadays, there exist other methods of human reproduction, for example artificial insemination. This is where sperm is injected into the vagina by artificial means (that is, not by a penis). The problem with using the word artificial in this context is that it reinforces the view of intercourse as natural or normal sex. For this reason the term donor insemination (DI) is preferred.

With or without medical help, lesbians are clearly capable of using donor insemination as a method of becoming pregnant. Recently in Britain there have been attempts to prevent single women (lesbian or heterosexual) obtaining donor insemination by making it illegal for clinics to offer such services. Although such attempts subsequently failed, the emphasis on the importance of the family as the two-parent, heterosexual, nuclear family was not lost. Section 13 of the Human Fertilisation and Embryology Act 1990 states that a woman should not have access to certain treatments for infertility including donor insemination, 'unless account has been taken of the welfare of any child who may be born as a result of the treatment (*including the need of that child for a father*)' [my emphasis]. The controversy over the so-called 'virgin births', reported widely in Britain early in 1991, also illustrated the resistance which exists to women seeking to become mothers outside marriage and, in this case, without ever having had intercourse with a man. In such a political climate it is significant that the British Pregnancy Advisory Service, which has been one of the few clinics prepared to provide donor insemination to lesbians and single women over the last ten years, decided to end its donor insemination service a few months later.

Prevented from obtaining treatment at a licensed clinic, lesbians could self-inseminate with donated sperm. In the past many lesbians have preferred to carry out insemination for themselves rather than via the medical profession, which generally regards donor insemination as a way of helping heterosexual couples conceive a child. However, more recently, self-insemination choices for lesbians have been affected by AIDS (Richardson, 1989). In clinics donors are screened for infection with HIV before their sperm is used. The alternative of self-insemination involves trusting a known donor and/or accepting some risk of possible infection with HIV. (For a more detailed discussion of artificial insemination and AIDS, see page 91.)

Apart from the assumption that it is unlikely, if not impossible, that a woman will become pregnant if she is a lesbian, the notion that a woman cannot be a lesbian and a mother is also strengthened by the view that lesbians do not want children. Once again this highlights the contradiction between the belief in a natural maternal instinct in all women and the expectation that such instincts will be expressed only within a heterosexual, preferably married, relationship. To some extent this contradiction has been avoided by stereotyping lesbians as women who are essentially masculine and unlike other 'real' women in their interests and desires.

Following the publicity given to contested custody cases, donor insemination for lesbians and, more recently, 'virgin births', it has become increasingly clear that lesbian mothers do exist. This challenge to the belief that lesbians should not and cannot be mothers has been resisted. This is evidenced in a number of ways: the media has frequently portrayed lesbian motherhood as something sensational; many doctors and social workers are unwilling to offer information and services to lesbians wanting to become pregnant or wishing to adopt or foster a child; and the courts are reluctant to grant custody or access to lesbian mothers. The State also discriminates against lesbian motherhood in Britain through such provisions as Section 28 of the 1988 Local Government Act, which makes it illegal for local authorities to promote the teaching in schools of 'the acceptability of homosexuality as a *pretended* family relationship' [my emphasis], and Section 13 of the Human Fertilisation and Embryology Act 1990.

Behind these actions lies the assumption that lesbians do not make good mothers, based on a concern that being brought up by a lesbian would be harmful or damaging to a child. What is meant by this is revealed, for example, in the conditions imposed by the courts. When a lesbian mother does win custody or access, she might well find that restrictions are placed on her lifestyle (Richardson, 1981a). The courts may recommend that if she is a lesbian a mother should do everything in her power to ensure that her children do not grow up to be lesbian or gay themselves. This could mean the courts making access or custody conditional on the mother not telling her children she is a lesbian; not mixing with other lesbians; not being open about her lesbianism; not getting involved with groups concerned with the rights of lesbians; and not living with or having sexual relationships with other women. In one case a mother was asked to sign a formal under-taking that she would not sleep with her lover while her son was staying with them, would hide any literature on homosexuality, and would never mention the subject in her son's presence (Rights of Women Lesbian Custody Group, 1986).

The kind of court-ordered restrictions I have mentioned are likely to cause emotional and possibly financial problems for the lesbian mother and her children (Rand *et al.*, 1982). Preventing a lesbian from living with her lover by making custody or access contingent upon not cohabiting may make her extremely unhappy, and this may well have an adverse effect on her relationship with the children. It may also lead to a woman suffering social and economic problems as a single parent. Also, if a woman is ordered by the court not to mix with other lesbians, or to give up her involvement in lesbian/feminist politics, this is likely to have the negative effect of isolating her from crucial sources of support and self-esteem.

Public concern with lesbian motherhood has prompted researchers to examine the psychological effects on children of growing up in a lesbian household, the idea being that if it can be proven that such an upbringing is not harmful, then society ought not to discriminate against lesbian mothers. What researchers have failed to ask is what children might gain from being brought up by lesbians. The evidence is that children, especially girls, being brought up in a lesbian household are at far less risk of sexual abuse than children raised in a household with a male parent present. The majority of cases of sexual abuse in the home are by fathers towards daughters. Also, the experience of difference need not be negative. As one lesbian mother commented:

> My son meets so many friends, women and men, that he's never been nervous about strangers and always seems part of a big family. I think he'll grow up to be much more tolerant as well as confident, accepting people's differences and appreciating individual qualities. I see his life enriched by the way we live. (Shapiro, 1987, pp. 51–2).

The question most often asked is what effect does a lesbian mother have on her children's psychosexual development? Will they copy their mother's example and grow up lesbian or gay?

There is no evidence that children raised by lesbians are any more likely to become lesbian or gay than are children living in a heterosexual family. After all, most lesbians and gay men are the children of heterosexual parents. Studies carried out so far suggest that children raised by lesbian mothers tend to grow up with predominantly heterosexual interests (Golombok *et al.*, 1983).

This ought not to matter. Lesbians should not have to prove that their children develop into 'happy heterosexuals' in order to be considered fit to bring up children. To expect this is to accept a view of lesbianism and gay relationships as negative and undesirable, and as such is yet another form of lesbian and gay oppression. Furthermore, it ignores the fact that, in common with many heterosexual women, a significant number of lesbians do not want their children to grow up to accept, unquestioningly, a heterosexual world with its gender inequalities and culturally imposed definitions of femininity and masculinity. As Pat, a mother of two small children, says:

> It's terrible really when I think about it. In order to keep my children I had to agree to bring them up to be heterosexual whatever that means, and I ask myself what does that say about being gay, which I am. And what happens if my kids do decide to have gay relationships? It's not on is it? Not seen as a viable option.

A further worry that is often raised about granting custody to lesbian mothers is that children may be picked on or teased at school, even to the extent of losing their friends. On this basis the less open about her lesbianism a woman is, or is willing to agree to become, the more likely it is she will be granted custody or access. There is no evidence to suggest that, as a group, children of lesbian mothers get picked on significantly more than other children. Children are teased for all sorts of reasons – for being too fat, too small, too thin, wearing glasses and, more seriously, for being mentally or physically disabled or belonging to an ethnic minority group. Yet no one would seriously consider this a reason for taking these children away from their parents. It might be more helpful to question the kind of society which victimizes people who are in any way different from what is generally thought of as the norm. If children do experience social rejection or teasing we ought to regard this as an argument for an end to anti-lesbianism, rather than as a valid reason for denying lesbians the right to parenthood.

Clearly it is difficult for lesbians to choose motherhood. Although as women they are likely to be strongly socialized into wanting children, popular beliefs about lesbianism inform them they are not fit to be mothers. This is a view which is reinforced by the limits to choice that society imposes on them, in denying those who already have children the right to bring them up, and in failing to provide information, support and resources to enable those who wish to become mothers to do so. Given these constraints, it is hardly surprising if many lesbians feel they do not want children. Yet more and more women are questioning the assumption that they must choose between lesbianism and motherhood. The development of lesbian/feminist movements over the last two decades has been crucial to this. Not only have they helped women to regard lesbian motherhood as a choice they might make, but they have also helped to make it more of a reality by actively campaigning for an end to discrimination against lesbians, including the pressures on them to concede their rights to parenthood. It is only through perceiving motherhood as a possibility which they have both the right and the resources to be able to choose that lesbians are likely to construct a desire for maternity.

Infertility

Apart from those women who do not have children because society makes it very hard for them to do so, women may also be denied the choice to have children through infertility. Approximately one in eight couples and an unknown proportion of lesbians and single heterosexual women are infertile. Yet, generally speaking, most women do not expect to be infertile. Finding out that you are can therefore come as a shock, especially if a woman has already decided that she wants children.

Such expectations – of being able to have children – are reflected in discussions about the choice to have or not to have children, where the assumption is almost always that it is possible to have them. Similarly, feminism has mainly been concerned with helping women to achieve control over fertility through contraception and abortion. Yet this is only one aspect of reproductive freedom. Having the right to choose depends also on those women who want to have children being able to do so. What happens when a woman decides to have a child and then finds that either she or her partner is infertile? What 'choices' are available to women in these circumstances?

One option is to seek a cure for infertility. This can be a slow and emotionally difficult process to go through (Pfeffer and Woolett, 1983). To determine the cause of infertility a woman may have to undergo many different tests over a period of months, sometimes years, before a diagnosis is made. In most cases of infertility it is assumed that it is the woman who has the problem. (Even when it is known that the man is infertile, a woman may be expected to 'protect' the man.) In fact, in about a third of all cases defective sperm is the cause. In women, failure to ovulate is often the problem. Damage or blockage to the fallopian tubes is another very common reason for failure to conceive.

Even if a woman eventually does find out what is stopping her from becoming or staying pregnant, which is by no means always the case, there is no guarantee that the treatment she may be offered will work. Doctors may suggest surgery to repair blocked fallopian tubes; fertility drugs to induce ovulation; sex education or counselling; donor insemination to bypass male infertility or, possibly, one of the new reproductive technologies. The chances of success vary with each of these, and with different individuals receiving treatment. The highest degree of success is currently with hormonal disorders, such as failure to ovulate or infertility resulting from failure of the embryo to become implanted in the uterine wall. Under these circumstances fertility drugs can be used to stimulate the ovaries to produce eggs. With the drug clomiphene, ovulation can be induced in about 40 per cent of women who have never started or have stopped having periods, and in about 80 per cent of women whose periods are infrequent and irregular. Of those who do manage to ovulate as a result of having taken fertility drugs, less than half are likely to conceive.

A woman's decision to take drugs such as clomiphene will be affected by what else she knows about their use besides how effective they are. Drugs used in the treatment of infertility can have undesirable side-effects. Clomiphene can cause hot flushes, abdominal pain, blurred vision, headaches, dizziness, enlargement of the ovaries and multiple births. Many women are also concerned about whether taking fertility drugs will have any long-term effects on their health. Although no statistical link has been established, some doctors believe there may be a possible association between taking certain fertility drugs and ovarian cancer.

In addition to what she knows about infertility and its treatment, a woman's ability to have a child will be limited by the access she has to the various forms of infertility treatment currently available. It is the medical profession who decide who is eligible for treatment and, generally speaking, this means heterosexual, preferably married, couples. Even then a doctor may be unwilling or unable, because of government cuts in spending, to offer certain forms of treatment. In such cases treatment is limited to those who can afford and are willing to pay for it. This is particularly true of some of the more recent developments in reproductive technology. *In vitro* fertilization, for example, is not at present widely available in Britain on the National Health Service and can be very costly, with no way of knowing how many cycles of treatment may be needed before pregnancy results. The 'success' rate of IVF is notoriously low: in the UK it is reported to be about 10 per cent or less (see p. 92).

To decide to keep on trying in the hope that one day you will conceive is a choice which demands certain resources, not least an enormous commitment to wanting a child. For different reasons, so does the decision to try and adopt. The process of adoption can be long, painful and is very often unsuccessful. Partly because of the easier availability of contraception and abortion, and partly because many more women are raising children on their own, there are fewer babies available for adoption than there are people who would like to adopt. This means that the choice of adoption is restricted to those whom adoption agencies feel will make the best adoptive parents. Once again it would seem that traditional beliefs about motherhood and the family are paramount. Although single women and men can legally adopt a child, only a very small proportion of adoptions in Britain are by single people. Lesbians and gay men, who can only adopt as single parents not as lesbian or gay couples, are likely to find adoption (and fostering) extremely difficult, especially if they are open about their sexuality (Skeates and Jabri, 1988). One indicator of this is the attempt in Britain to prevent lesbian and gay men from being foster parents. In December 1990 the government issued a draft of its guidelines to the 1989 Children Act. Paragraph 16 of the draft specifically targeted 'gays':

> It would be wrong arbitrarily to exclude any particular groups of people from consideration (as suitable foster parents). But the chosen way of life of some adults may mean that they would not be able to provide a suitable environment for the care and nurture of a child. No one has a 'right' to be a foster parent. *Equal rights' and 'gay rights' policies have no place in fostering services.* [my emphasis]

In response to professional and public opinion the final version of the guidelines was changed and the highlighted sentence removed. However this should not be taken to mean that fostering will necessarily be any easier in future for lesbians and gay men.

A prospective adoptive or foster parent must also be deemed able to afford to provide a child with what she needs materially as well as emotionally. In a society which expects high standards of material, as well as emotional, support for children, this is restrictive for the poor, the young and the unemployed. Nor are these groups likely to be able to afford, should they so desire, to adopt a baby from abroad. The National Association for the Childless, for example, initiated a scheme to help their members adopt children from Colombia. Although it is illegal to buy children in Britain, travel and other costs amounting to several thousands of pounds are paid by the adoptive parents.

Clearly for many women, adoption will be difficult, if not impossible. They could always choose to accept not being able to have children of their own, but coming to terms with infertility can be very hard in a society which puts such an emphasis on women wanting and being able to have children, especially if they are married. This is exemplified by the negative way that women who are infertile are generally regarded. They are often labelled as barren, sterile, childless, women to be pitied. Such interpretations are likely to influence the way in which women themselves experience their inability to conceive. They may, for example, feel worthless, ashamed, inadequate, and a failure as a real woman. This is especially likely where a woman views having children as a central aspect of how she sees herself and her future, a view which society strongly encourages by defining women who marry and have children as more mature, adult, responsible and feminine than women who do neither of these. The extent to which individual women experience these pressures is likely to vary according to 'race' and class. For instance, in some cultures more than others a woman's status is measured in terms of the number of children she has.

If the idea of women not having children was socially more acceptable, then infertility would no longer be regarded as such a problem, nor would the infertile have as great a need for their own pressure groups. This and other issues relating to infertility will be discussed in more detail in the following chapter.

5

Reproductive technologies

The debate surrounding the new reproductive technologies has mainly been concerned with their ethical, legal and medical implications. Not enough has been said about how such developments might affect women's lives, despite the fact that the new technology has great significance for women. Besides affecting our rights, obligations and abilities to be mothers, it poses a radical challenge to many of the basic assumptions about reproduction and sexuality.

Feminist discussion of the new medical interventions into reproduction has looked at what effects these developments are likely to have from women's points of view; in particular it has asked who controls the new technologies, who is eligible to use them and what are they being used for? Will they aid women's liberation or will they further their oppression? (See, for example, Arditti *et al.*, 1984; Corea *et al.*, 1985; Corea, 1988; Hanmer, 1981, 1992; Klein, 1989; Stanworth, 1987.) Much feminist writing comes to the latter conclusion. Among some of the criticisms made are that the new reproductive technologies are being used to uphold traditional notions of motherhood and femininity, have serious eugenic implications, have a low success rate and are expensive, most pose health risks to women and, most importantly, they can be seen as extending control over women's reproductive activities. Such concerns have led some feminists to resist the new developments in reproductive technology. The Feminist International Network of Resistance to Reproductive and Genetic Engineering (FINRRAGE), set up in 1984, involves women in this way. Others take a more optimistic view, arguing that the new reproductive technologies are not necessarily bad for women and should not be rejected totally (see, for example, Birke *et al.*, 1990). This chapter aims to provide an introduction to some of the recent developments in reproductive technology and to assess their possible consequences for women.

Artificial insemination

Each year several thousand babies are born in Britain as a result of artificial insemination. This is a simple procedure: a syringe or similar object is used to introduce sperm into the vagina or cervix around the time a woman is ovulating. As a reproductive technique, therefore, artificial insemination is no more (some might say less) complicated than vaginal intercourse; something women could do themselves without the help of doctors or a clinic providing they have access to a sperm donor.

Simple though the procedure may be, in practice artificial insemination usually occurs within a medical setting. It is available on the National Health Service primarily as a way of overcoming male infertility in marriage. When the husband's sperm is used – for example, if it is felt that the chances of pregnancy would be increased by concentrating his semen or by inserting it directly into the uterus – this is termed Artificial Insemination by Husband (AIH). When semen from a donor is used – for example, if the husband is infertile or suffers from a serious hereditary disease – this is often referred to as Artificial Insemination by Donor (AID). For reasons I have previously outlined, the term donor insemination (DI) will be used instead.

The distinction between AIH and AID is one which not only medicine, but the church and the law also seek to make. Generally speaking, opposition is not to insemination by husband but to insemination by donor. The Roman Catholic church is opposed to donor insemination and the Jewish faith considers it a violation of the marriage bond. Those who are morally opposed to artificial insemination by husband argue that it is unnatural, and that sex and reproduction should not be separated. The procedure also requires the man to produce semen by masturbation, which in some religious communities is still considered to be a sin.

The Warnock Committee was appointed by the British government in 1982 to consider the social, ethical and legal implications of the new developments in reproductive technology, including the not-so-new techniques of AID and AIH. The committee's main proposal was that a statutory licensing authority be established to monitor and control developments in reproductive technology. The Warnock Committee published their report outlining their recommendations in 1984, but it was not until 1987 that the government in a White Paper outlined its proposals for legislation on issues dealt with in the Report. The Human Fertilisation and Embryology Act finally became law in 1990, eight long years after Warnock was first set up. The Act created a Human Fertilisation and Embryology Authority, which replaced the Voluntary Licensing Authority which had been operating since 1985.

The Warnock Report made a distinction between AIH and AID: it recommended that DI should be legally regulated but saw no reason for controlling artificial insemination by husband. Under the present legal system in Britain, it is illegal to offer DI as a service without a licence. There have also been changes in the law regarding the status of DI children. If the woman is married, or treated with a man as a couple, then the man, as long as he consents to the insemination, is legally the father of the child. The donor is not legally regarded as the father of the child and, consequently, if a single woman conceives by DI the child is legally fatherless. Previously the law considered children born by donor insemination to be illegitimate. Strictly speaking, the child should have been registered as 'father unknown' and the mother and her husband could then apply to adopt. In practice, however, it was commonly accepted that most married couples who had a DI baby would (illegally) register the child in the husband's name.

From a feminist perspective this is a complex issue. The change in the law represents a challenge to definitions of fatherhood which have traditionally emphasised the importance of men's biological rather than their social contribution to parenthood. Despite this, many feminists were against proposals to change the law. Apart from asking why women on their own cannot legitimize their children, their concern is that such changes represent an extension of men's rights, and hence male control, over women and children (Sutton and Friedman, 1982). Unmarried men are being given the same rights to children as married men.

Other debates surrounding donor insemination centre upon

whether or not a child conceived by this method should be told of her origins. Both the British Agencies for Adoption and Fostering and the British Association of Social Workers have argued that children born through donor insemination should have similar rights to adopted children: a right to know, in this case, who their genetic father was. Provision is made in law for a child, on reaching eighteen and after receiving counselling, to find out whether they were conceived by DI and if they would or might be related to a prospective spouse, and any other information the Licensing Authority is required to give (not specified). The Warnock Report concluded that children should have access to basic information about the donor's ethnic origin and genetic health. But the committee did not feel that a child should be allowed to know the name of the donor. The report states that donors should remain anonymous both to those using donor insemination and to DI children themselves; nor should the donor know who uses his sperm (Warnock Report, 1984). This latter recommendation has potentially important implications for single heterosexual women and lesbians, whose access to DI and rights over their DI children might otherwise be threatened. The Warnock Committee were not, however, concerned with supporting the use of DI for lesbians and single women. On the contrary, the report defined DI primarily in terms of a medical treatment for male infertility.

Donor insemination need not be seen only as a way of helping heterosexual couples conceive a child. Insemination by donor has also been used by lesbians and single heterosexual women who choose to have children without having vaginal intercourse with men. Another reason why some lesbians may prefer to have a DI baby is to try to ensure undisputed guardianship and custody of their child. This is understandable given the court's reluctance to grant custody and access to lesbian mothers in disputed custody cases (see page 80).

In the past there has been resistance to lesbians using DI to have children. In 1978 there was a public outcry in Britain when it was 'revealed' that a London doctor had helped a number of lesbians to become pregnant using this method. With few exceptions the press responded in a manner that was both sensationalizing and anti-lesbian. It was described as 'scandalous', 'horrific' and 'outrageous' that such a thing had been allowed to happen (Hemmings, 1980).

In response to such criticisms the British Medical Association, the following year, proposed that doctors should be prohibited from helping lesbians become pregnant by DI, on the grounds that it would be medically unethical. This proposal was defeated by a narrow majority of 162 to 148. This did not mean that the BMA favoured the use of donor insemination for lesbians. The BMA's main concern was to uphold the rights of doctors to have freedom of conscience to do as they saw fit for their patients. In no way was the decision directly supportive of the rights of lesbians to have children.

Although some lesbians and single heterosexual women have been successful in obtaining donor insemination, the view that DI is primarily a treatment for male infertility his limited its medical use in Britain to mainly heterosexual couples. The Warnock Report and subsequent legislation endorses this position. In the 1960s the concerns expressed about DI were that it threatened the basis of marriage and monogamy, the importance of inheritance through the male line, and religious objections to masturbation. DI within marriage is now seen as relatively 'normal'; in the nineties the concern has shifted to the use of DI by single women and lesbians (see page 78).

These are not, however, the only choices open to women. A woman does not have to be limited by what her doctor or the fertility clinic thinks about her desire to have a child by DI. Providing a donor is available this is something women can do for themselves. Having said that, however, it is not clear whether the criminalization of non-licensed DI services will affect women's self-insemination choices. (For a discussion of the practicalities of carrying out self-insemination, see Saffron, 1987.) There are several reasons why a woman may prefer to self-inseminate. First of all, it allows a woman a greater amount of control over the process of insemination. It also means that she can choose a known donor. While many do not, some women do want their child to know the father. Also, the cost of using a clinic may be prohibitive for some women.

In recent years the choice to self-inseminate has been affected by AIDS. No cases of HIV infection due to donor insemination have so far been reported in the UK. However in 1985 four Australian women were reported to have become infected through DI. As clinics now screen would-be donors for HIV infection, the risk is to women carrying out self-insemination. This is why some lesbians and single heterosexual women (those who can afford it), who would otherwise have opted for self-insemination, now prefer to receive DI through a clinic. Ironically, the introduction of stronger medical and legal control over donor insemination is likely to make it difficult for lesbians and single heterosexual women to be inseminated through a clinic, which could put both them and any children they might have at possible future risk of HIV infection if they self-inseminate. (For a more detailed discussion of AIDS and donor insemination, see Richardson, 1989.)

Test-tube babies

The world's first IVF or 'test-tube' baby, Louise Brown, was born in Britain in 1978. Her birth was the result of research carried out by two doctors, Patrick Steptoe and Robert Edwards, who pioneered the use of *in vitro* fertilization (IVF).

IVF is used mainly to overcome female infertility due to the fallopian tubes, down which the egg must pass to reach the uterus, being damaged, diseased or absent. It may also be used to treat other forms of infertility, for instance where a woman does not produce eggs, by using donated eggs.

The concept of IVF is quite simple. A woman is given hormones to stimulate ovulation so that several eggs are produced during the monthly cycle. The ripe eggs are then removed surgically from her ovary and put into a laboratory dish with live sperm so that fertilization can occur. Once cell division has begun the fertilized egg (embryo) is transferred back to the woman's uterus. There it may implant itself in the lining of her womb and continue to develop normally. IVF means, therefore, the fertilization of an egg outside, rather than inside, a woman's body. Gamete intra-fallopian tube transfer (GIFT) is a variation of IVF: in this case eggs are placed in the fallopian tube with sperm, so that fertilization takes place there rather than in a 'test-tube'.

Though simple in theory, in practice IVF is a complicated procedure and requires very precise timing and carefully controlled conditions if it is to result in pregnancy. Very often implantation does not occur, and overall IVF has a low success rate. In the UK the success rate for live births per treatment cycle is around

10 per cent or less (ILA, 1989): that is, only one woman in ten who undergoes IVF will have a child. At some clinics their chances may be even lower. One way of trying to increase the chances of a successful pregnancy is to return more than one embryo after fertilization, in the hope that at least one of these will attach itself in the uterus. The risk in doing this is that a woman may have more than one child. For this reason the authority regulating treatment in Britain suggests that no more than three embryos should be placed in a woman at any one time.

IVF can be a very stressful procedure to go through. After having an operation to remove ripe eggs, a woman must wait to find out the outcome of each stage of the process. Will the eggs be fertilized? Will they implant if put back? Will there be only one baby or several? In addition to the physical and mental stresses this may cause, IVF is also financially very costly, with no way of assessing how many cycles of treatment may be needed before pregnancy results. Given that it is, so far, relatively difficult to obtain IVF on the National Health Service, this limits its use to those who can afford and are accepted for treatment.

As with other reproductive technologies, access to treatment is controlled by the law and the medical profession. This was made abundantly clear in Britain in 1987 when a woman was not allowed on the IVF programme at a Manchester hospital. The doctors involved decided that the woman and her husband would not be 'suitable' parents. The woman challenged the decision in the High Court and lost. The current legal position on access to IVF is similar to that for donor insemination. Whilst it is not a criminal offence under the 1990 Act to provide IVF to single women (and lesbians), clinics must consider the welfare of the child before going ahead and, specifically, the need for a father.

In addition to sexual identity and marital status, a woman's skin colour, age and social class are all likely to affect her chances of being selected as fit to become a mother and deserving of treatment. Women entering IVF programmes must demonstrate what are deemed to be appropriate psychological as well as social characteristics for motherhood. In practice this means that the 'choice' to have IVF is likely to be largely restricted to young(ish) white women in stable heterosexual relationships who are accepted for, and can afford, treatment.

IVF draws attention to a number of important social issues.

Why do women want to become genetic/biological mothers? What do we mean by the word 'mother'? Why is it those women such as poor women, Black women, single women and lesbians whose reproductive choices are limited? IVF is also important because it makes possible other reproductive interventions. One of the most controversial of these is surrogate motherhood.

Surrogate motherhood

This is an expression which has several different meanings. It has been used to describe the situation where a woman who produces normal egg cells but is unable to bear a child (perhaps because she has a history of miscarriages, is physically disabled or has no uterus) has an egg fertilized by IVF and then transferred to the uterus of another woman who 'carries' the pregnancy for her. When the baby is born the woman who has given birth to the child, the surrogate mother, is expected to give the child to its genetic mother to bring up. This practice is sometimes called 'womb-leasing'.

A variation on this practice is egg donation. In this case, instead of lending or 'leasing' her womb, a woman donates an egg to another woman. This technique might be used where a woman can bear a child but is unable to produce eggs, or is advised not to use her own eggs because she might pass on a serious hereditary condition to her child. The donated egg may be fertilized by IVF or through donor insemination. In the latter case the initial stages of the embryo's development will take place in the uterus of the woman donating the egg, before the embryo is washed out in a process called *lavage* and transferred to the uterus of the woman who will bear the child. Three people will have contributed to the making of a baby: the woman who donated the egg, the man whose sperm was used to fertilize the egg, and the woman who developed and gave birth to the baby. In this situation the person who is labelled the surrogate mother is the woman who donated the egg (that is, the child's genetic mother) and not, as in the previous case, the person who bore the child for nine months.

The most commonly practised form of surrogate motherhood is where the person who is called the surrogate mother donates both her egg and her uterus to enable another woman to be a

mother. This requires none of the complicated medical interventions of IVF or embryo transfer. The surrogate mother
becomes pregnant either through vaginal intercourse with the
father or through donor insemination with his sperm and, providing this is successful, agrees to hand over the baby after she has
given birth to it nine months later.

In Britain surrogate mothers have been hired by an agency
linked to the National Centre for Surrogate Parents based in the
United States. This led to the birth, on 4 January 1985, of Britain's
first commercial surrogate baby, Baby Cotton, for a reported fee
of £13 000. The surrogate mother received only half of this, the
remainder going to the surrogate agency. The publicity which
surrounded the birth prompted Social Services immediately to
seek a place of safety order, preventing the removal of the child,
a girl, from the hospital. This meant that the couple who had paid
for and wanted the child could not claim her. The only way the
child's father could get the baby was to apply for her to be made
a ward of court and trust he would eventually be given custody.
This he did, and within a week he and his wife were granted care
and control of the child. They subsequently flew to the United
States and out of the jurisdiction of the British courts.

Baby Cotton was not the first baby to be born of a surrogate
mother in Britain. It was the commercialization of surrogate
arrangements which prompted the furore over the birth of Baby
Cotton. Undoubtedly, what also lay behind much oι the public
outcry was a belief in the existence of a special bond between a
woman and the baby she has nurtured for nine months. 'How
could she?' was the question many people asked. What natural,
normal woman would want to do such a thing? Critics of surrogate
motherhood talked about the psychological risks involved to the
surrogate mother, who might end up feeling guilt, regret or loss.

The government's reaction to the public outcry surrounding the
Cotton case was quickly to draft the 1985 Surrogacy Arrangements
Act. The Act does not criminalize all surrogacy arrangements,
it only bans surrogate arrangements negotiated by commercial
agencies. The law does not prohibit doctors or voluntary agencies
from introducing a surrogate to would-be parents free of charge,
or parents from paying a fee to the surrogate. However it is illegal
to advertise to be a surrogate or to find a surrogate, even if it is
not a commercial arrangement.

In any other situation a woman who conceives a child and then gives birth to it is called the child's natural mother, even if she decides not to keep the child and offers it up for adoption. Surrogate motherhood therefore demands that we re-examine the way we think about motherhood. What do we mean when we talk about a child's 'real' mother? Do we mean the person who rears the child and is, in a social sense, the child's mother? Do we mean the person who bore the child for nine months and gave birth to her? Or do we mean the person who is genetically related to the child?

Some indication lies in the response to different forms of surrogate motherhood. For instance, the Warnock Report approved egg donation but rejected surrogate motherhood where it involved one woman selling, renting or giving the use of her uterus to another. The reason for this distinction is not difficult to understand. In our society childrearing and childbearing are closely associated. It is generally assumed that the person who gives birth to the child will also be the person who looks after it. Surrogate motherhood, insofar as it involves one person who bears the child and another who proposed to be the child's eventual mother, challenges this association and thereby threatens those structures, both social and psychological, which ensure that it is women and not men who have primary responsibility for childcare. In this sense one might ask, will acceptance of surrogacy help to break down traditional beliefs about the family and motherhood? This is an interesting question, but we also need to consider whether, under current legal and medical control, it is more likely that surrogacy will be used in ways that will strengthen the traditional beliefs.

Egg donation, because the woman who wants a baby is both the bearing and the eventual mother, does not pose a similar threat to the institution of motherhood and the organization of childcare. Nevertheless the Warnock Report did disapprove of one method of egg donation, where the initial stages of the embryo's development take place in the donor's uterus and the embryo is then washed out and transferred to the uterus of the woman who will eventually give birth to the child and be its mother.

The Warnock Report insisted, and it is now the case under British law, that a woman who gives birth to a child should be regarded as the legal mother. If a surrogate mother had a child for a woman the child is legally the surrogate mother's, no matter whose egg was used. The eventual mother would have to adopt the child legally, even if she was the genetic mother. (This would be difficult where a man was not involved, whose child it was genetically, as private adoption is illegal in Britain.) If the surrogate mother wanted to keep the child and not give it up for adoption she would have the legal right. This is further strengthened by the fact that, under the Surrogacy Arrangements Act, surrogacy contracts are unenforceable and, therefore, adoption by the commissioning parents cannot be guaranteed.

In the United States surrogate contracts have been enforced in some states, challenging the institution of motherhood. In the celebrated Stern versus Whitehead case in 1987 the surrogate mother, Mary Beth Whitehead, lost her attempt to keep the baby she had borne, and which was genetically hers, Baby M. Even though the contract was declared illegal, in the eyes of the law the child's father, Bill Stern, had a legal right to challenge and ultimately to win custody of the child. Apparently, in the eyes of the law, the facts of the conception were considered more important than the facts of the process of pregnancy and birth. In another case in the United States a couple contracted a woman to have a fertilized egg develop in her uterus and to give birth to the resulting child. The court decided that the surrogate mother should not be registered on the birth certificate as the child's mother. The child's legal mother was found to be the genetic and eventual mother, not the surrogate mother who gave birth to the child (WRRIC, 1987).

There is no one single feminist line on the issues raised by recent developments in reproductive technology, but rather a variety of arguments and positions. Some feminists campaign against reproductive techniques such as IVF, because they belief that, firmly under medical control and used mainly to support the family, they are likely to lead to women being further exploited and to the loss of even more control over our own bodies (see, for example, Arditti *et al.*, 1984; Corea *et al.*, 1985; Corea, 1988; Klein, 1989). Many women in the past have been obliged to sell their bodies for sex, now for similar reasons they may end up selling their bodies for reproductive purposes. From this perspective, Andrea

Dworkin has suggested that surrogate motherhood can be regarded as a new form of female prostitution (Dworkin, 1983).

Whatever one thinks about such possibilities, the potential for exploitation clearly exists, especially in the case of Black and Third World women. John Stehura, President of the Bionetics Foundation in California, demonstrated this when he claimed that a 'Third World' woman would not even need to be healthy to become a surrogate mother; nor, he implied, would she need to be paid as much as other (white) women:

> If we could cross international lines, then $1000 is a significant sum of money whereas [in the US] it's just a week's or a month's wages. . . . The [Third World] mother could have a health problem which could be quite serious. However, if her diet is good and other aspects of her life are OK she could become a viable mother for genuine embryo transfer. (*Guardian*, 3 July 1984)

In the case of surrogacy which involves egg donation (rather than a woman being hired to go through with the pregnancy and birth) the situation is different, though potentially still exploitative. Because the egg donors are genetically related to the babies produced, the purchasers are likely to want only certain kinds of women. Since it is mainly white, middle-class couples who can afford to pay for surrogacy arrangements, what surrogacy firms are likely to want are healthy white women to act as egg donors. However there is still social class to consider; it is still likely to mean working class women serving the higher social classes and men.

Other feminists are also concerned with male control of reproductive technology, the health risks of certain reproductive technologies and the possibilities for the exploitation of women. These feminists, however, take a more optimistic view, arguing for more infertility services to be available for women, and for women to have greater control over their development and use (see, for example, Birke *et al.*, 1990). They would, for instance, challenge the policy of offering new reproductive technologies to heterosexual couples only. This not only discriminates against lesbians, celibate and single heterosexual women who wish to have children by these methods, it also reinforces traditional beliefs about marriage and the family. New reproductive technologies are being used primarily to help married couples try to achieve what society expects of them, and to enable women to fulfil their supposed true destiny by helping them to have children. As Jalna Hanmer (1992) comments: 'Women rarely receive counselling on how a woman can have a fulfilling life without producing her own biological child.'

If women were not under such pressure to have children, at least within stable heterosexual relationships, infertility would not be considered to be such a problem. Feminists who argue that infertility services ought to be made more available acknowledge this, but they are also concerned to defend the right of all women to have children if they so wish (Pfeffer and Woollett, 1983).

Some feminists might also want to argue that, although the potential for exploitation undoubtedly exists, surrogate motherhood ought not to be rejected out of hand. For lesbian couples especially, surrogacy may be seen as an important development in so far as it makes it possible for both partners to contribute to the conception and the birth of a child. The egg of one woman could be fertilized and then transferred to the womb of her partner who would give birth to the child. The reason why some lesbians may desire this is that it would enable them to feel that the child was jointly theirs. As many women whose female partners have had children will know, co-parenting can be a difficult social reality to establish in a society which provides little support or validation for the lesbian family. A lesbian couple have no recognized relationship to each other, indeed the law in Britain defines a lesbian couple bringing up a child as a 'pretended family'. Also, if a lesbian has a child her partner, unless she has been appointed as the legal guardian, has no legally recognized relationship to the child they both care for. Having said that, it is clear that surrogacy is hardly the answer to the problem of recognition for lesbian families; nor would it directly challenge the privileged position of heterosexuality as the only socially and legally valid foundation for family life.

Eggs, embryos and sperm banks

The practice of artificial insemination has led to the setting-up of sperm banks where men can store their own sperm, for example before having a vasectomy, and where donated sperm can be kept. There are wide-ranging implications of being able to store sperm. In the United States, for example, there are agencies which offer sperm for sale, with the option of purchasing semen from donors with certain physical, social or racial characteristics. Guaranteed 'racially pure' sperm is a particular selling point, as is the occupational status of the male donor. The eugenic implications of this are clearly very worrying, especially in the context of present racial and class inequalities.

In Britain, where sperm is not yet marketed in this way, the social implications of freezing semen were discussed in the Warnock Report (1984). It approved sperm banks, but recommended that one of the licensing authority's functions should be to regulate the buying and selling of semen. Without a licence trading in sperm would be a criminal offence. The Warnock Report also approved the setting-up of frozen embryo banks, but again only on condition that similar safeguards were in operation to regulate their use. The freezing of eggs was not approved on the grounds that, unlike semen and embryos, eggs were not yet susceptible to safe and reliable storage processes.

Under the 1990 Act clinics require a licence to store sperm, eggs or embryos. The legal storage period for sperm and eggs is not more than ten years. Embryos should only be stored, with the consent of the donors, for a maximum of five years. The first baby produced from an embryo that had been frozen for several months before being implanted in a woman's uterus was born in March 1984 in Melbourne, Australia. Early the following year Britain's first 'frozen baby' was born.

One advantage to being able successfully to store embryos is that it may help to make IVF a less stressful procedure. Women trying to conceive a child by this method would not have to undergo further surgery to collect more eggs if, as is likely, their first attempt at becoming pregnant using IVF failed. Six or more eggs can be collected and fertilized in one operation, and since the code of practice suggests no more than three embryos should be implanted at any one time, the rest can be stored for possible future use.

Using IVF in this way raises questions about what should be done with embryos that are left over? This has evoked a great deal of comment from 'pro-life' organisations and supporters, who believe that from the moment of fertilization the embryo is a human being with a 'right-to-life'. Whilst objecting to the destruction of human embryos, they are opposed to storing them if it means that unused embryos will be kept for research and not implantation. Those who believe that research on embryos is necessary argue that it will increase knowledge about congenital diseases, miscarriages and infertility, help improve techniques of *in vitro* fertilization and contraception, and produce more effective methods of detecting gene or chromosome abnormalities.

The Warnock Report recommended that research on human embryos should be permitted up to fourteen days after fertilization (not counting any time during which the embryo may have been frozen). Some years later this became law in Britain with the passing of the 1990 Human Fertilisation and Embryology Act. Interestingly, not all the Warnock committee members had been in agreement with this recommendation. There was a dissenting report, supported by anti-abortion groups like Life and The Society for the Protection of the Unborn Child, which opposed any experimentation on embryos and argued that embryos created by *in vitro* fertilization should only be used for implanting in women; any other use should be a criminal offence. The debate over embryo research prompted, in 1985, Enoch Powell's Unborn Child (Protection) Bill. Had it become law, the Powell Bill would have banned research on human embryos and placed restrictions on the practice of IVF. In so far as it would have entitled embryos to legal protection as 'unborn children', it would have also threatened abortion rights.

Anti-abortionists oppose embryo research for the same reasons as they oppose abortion, because they believe that the embryo and the foetus have a 'right-to-life'. For different reasons some feminists are also opposed to embryo research, whilst upholding the rights of women to abortion. Their concern is that the development of a market in human embryos could lead to women being exploited as egg donors (Corea *et al.*, 1985). Some feminists are also concerned about the possible eugenic implications of embryo research, for instance that research on genetic disorders will lead to attempts to make all babies 'perfect', or the creation of human beings with pre-determined characteristics by genetic manipulation of embryos (Hanmer, 1992).

There are also concerns about the relative rights of women and men to a frozen embryo. The rights of men in relation to children have been strengthened in recent years, for instance by legislation giving unmarried men similar rights to their children as married men, and individual men are now demanding more control over whether or not 'their' children can be born. There have been cases where men have gone to court to try to stop a woman having an abortion (see page 73) and cases where men have claimed rights over frozen embryos. For example, in a divorce case in the United States a custody action was fought over seven frozen embryos. The woman wanted to use the embryos in an attempt to have children, and her husband refused. Although the judge eventually awarded custody of the embryos to the woman, the decision was based on the embryo's rights, that is, the 'right-to-life' argument. Such thinking regards the woman and the embryo as distinct entities. The embryo (or foetus) becomes an independent subject whose interests need protecting; embryos are given an existence 'independent of the maternal environment even though they cannot at the present time become a child without it' (Hanmer, 1992). Feminists would argue that this split between the woman and the embryo, the severing of the relationship between the embryo and the womb, is an artificial one which disempowers women. From a feminist perspective the frozen embryo case could have been decided on the principle that the embryo is part of the mother's body and therefore hers to implant or not.

Being able to store embryos raises other important questions about motherhood. Theoretically embryo storage makes it possible to separate fertility from reproduction: a woman's choice to have a child need no longer be limited to a particular period of the lifespan, her fertile years. A woman could simply store her own eggs, or embryos, until she needed them for reproduction. Women who, because of their age or for other reasons, were unable to bear a child could have their embryos implanted in the uterus of a surrogate mother, who would bear the child. This would, of course, depend on surrogacy and embryo storage being both generally available and acceptable.

Such possible developments have radical implications for the way in which motherhood is usually thought of as a distinct period of women's lives: their 'childbearing years'. Separated from the need to be able to give birth, and with access to fertile eggs of their own throughout their lives using frozen storage, women could find motherhood becoming rather like fatherhood for men, a lifelong possibility. The freezing of eggs and embryos, as well as sperm, also makes it possible to extend parenthood even further, to beyond the grave. This has already happened in the case of women who have used their husband's frozen semen to conceive a child after his death. In France, attempts to prevent this happening led, in 1984, to one woman going to court to fight for the right to be inseminated with her dead husband's semen. A legal battle ensued which, eventually, she won. Will we in future witness men claiming the right to have children by a surrogate mother, using the frozen eggs or embryos of a dead partner?

If women could choose to become mothers at any stage of their lives what might the consequences be? The context in which women would choose motherhood would obviously be very different from what it is now. At present, many women feel they have to make up their minds whether or not to have a child during that period of their lives when becoming a mother seems most likely to stand in the way of their achieving other ambitions and desires. The possibility of being able to choose to have children at a later date might help to reduce this conflict between, in particular, paid work and motherhood. However, despite its superficial appeal, extending the possibility of having children to women past 'childbearing years' is hardly an answer to the problem of childcare, and would not directly challenge the reasons why women experience such conflicts in the first place.

The artificial womb

To most people the idea of growing babies in artificial incubators is pure science fiction, something that could only happen in novels such as Aldous Huxley's *Brave New World*, or Marge Piercy's *Woman on the Edge of Time*. It has, however, been suggested that we are closer than most of us realise to the artificial womb (Singer and Wells, 1984). Ectogenesis – the growth and development of a viable foetus outside a woman's uterus – is in part already possible. Neonatal intensive care units are pushing down the age at which babies born prematurely can be saved. Also, at the other end of the scale, research into *in vitro* fertilization has demonstrated that it is possible to grow embryos outside the womb.

The period during which a uterus is still necessary for foetal development has, then, already been reduced to less than twenty-two weeks of the nine months that pregnancy normally takes. If we continue to push back the age at which premature babies can be saved then, it has been claimed, we shall eventually reach the point at which a human embryo produced through IVF can be kept alive without ever putting it inside a woman's body (Singer and Wells, 1984).

It is improbable that this could ever happen in the foreseeable future, but just supposing it were possible to develop a human embryo outside a woman's body for the full nine months needed for development, ought we to do this?

Shulamith Firestone certainly thought so. In her book, *The Dialectic of Sex*, she argued that in order to become equal women needed to stop having children. The key to women's liberation was artificial reproduction. This was the technological means by which women could free themselves from the biological function of childbearing. To free women from this, Firestone argued, meant freedom from the family, the latter being a social unit organised around biological reproduction, and fundamentally oppressive to women (Firestone, 1971).

Firestone has been described as naive for failing to pay sufficient attention to the question of who controls the development of knowledge in science and technology and, also, how this knowledge is used (Rose and Hanmer, 1976). It is no use having technology to free women from those biological functions which may be oppressing them, if they do not have access to its use. A further criticism of her work is that it is not so much the biological fact of childbirth which oppresses women, and which we should therefore seek to eliminate, as the meanings attributed to this fact and the social, economic and psychological structures built upon those meanings. It is these, most feminists would argue, which need challenging, in particular the link between childbirth and childrearing.

Firestone did, very powerfully, draw attention to the revolutionary significance that reproductive technology might have for women. However under male supremacy the more immediate concern is how might reproductive technologies be used to gain greater control over women's lives and bodies? Whilst Firestone advocates the artificial womb as the answer to a maiden's prayer for liberation, others have warned that such developments could lead to the creation of a virtually all-male society where, except for a few 'queen bees' kept to produce eggs, women would be regarded as obsolete (Corea *et al.*, 1985).

Peter Singer and Deane Wells, like Firestone, take a more optimistic view. They argue that, if it were technologically possible, we ought to go ahead with ectogenesis for a number of reasons. These include freeing those women who so choose from the burdens of reproduction, the creation of a source of spare parts to replace diseased organs, and the elimination of the wastage of embryonic life caused by abortion (Singer and Wells, 1984).

This last suggestion is an interesting one. If we could keep a foetus alive outside a woman's body, and if terminations could be done using techniques that would not harm the foetus, then abortions would in effect become early births. Women could choose to end their pregnancies whilst preserving the foetus. At the moment an abortion inevitably means terminating the foetus, which leads to a confrontation between those who support a woman's right to choose and organizations such as Life and The Society for the Protection of the Unborn Child, which support the 'right-to-life' of the foetus. However, to assume that a separation of these 'rights' could lead to feminists and 'pro-life' supporters being able to 'embrace in happy harmony', as Singer and Wells suggest, seems equally futuristic!

Cloning

The development of IVF has made cloning in humans a possibility (cloning has already been achieved with certain species of animal, frogs for instance). Cloning involves splitting the embryo into separate cells, whilst it is in the earliest stages of cell division and consists of only two or four cells. Once separated each of these cells, if allowed to continue growing normally, will develop into a separate individual. These individuals will all be genetically identical and will look alike. This sometimes happens naturally in humans and when it does we call the clones identical twins.

The main argument against cloning from a feminist perspective is found in the answer to who, in a white, male-dominated society, would be cloned. Cloning could have similar social consequences as being able to choose the sex of one's baby: a society in which there were many more men than women and where male domination would be strengthened.

There is another form of cloning which may have rather different implications. With parthenogenesis, or 'virgin birth', the process governing cell division and growth of the embryo occurs without fertilization taking place: sperm is not needed. Because an egg-cell *is* necessary for reproduction to occur, men would not be able to reproduce themselves in this way. In this sense a world without men is biologically possible, whereas a world without women is not.

Recently it has been discovered that the start of this process of parthenogenesis, or asexual reproduction, can occur in humans. Although it is improbable that a baby will be born by this method of reproduction in the foreseeable future, this has not prevented speculation about what kind of a society might result if 'virgin births' were possible. One suggestion is that as women would be able to produce children by themselves, and since all the offspring of this form of reproduction would be female, this could eventually lead to an all-female society where men would be redundant (Cherfas and Gribbin, 1984). However as parthenogenesis is so potentially threatening to male domination and to individual men, even as science fiction, one would predict great resistance to research directed at making this technologically possible.

Choosing the sex of the child

It is not possible, at present, to conceive a child of the sex of one's choosing, although plenty of advice exists on how we might try to ensure we have a girl or a boy. One suggestion is that it might be possible to modify, or monitor, the environment of the vagina so that only X or Y sperm could fertilize an egg. (Each sperm has an X or a Y chromosome. If an X-carrying sperm fertilizes the egg-cell the embryo will develop into a female; fertilization with a Y-carrying sperm produces a male.) This is the principle behind much of the advice which suggests that the time of the month at which intercourse or insemination occurs can influence the probability of an X or a Y sperm fertilizing an egg. Certain other recommended methods of sex predetermination, such as douching or following a special diet, are also based on the belief that the vaginal environment – whether it is more or less acidic – may have a different effect on X and Y sperm, which in turn affects their survival or fertilizing capacity. The suggestion that whether or not a woman has an orgasm can influence what sex her child will be is also based on this principle.

One need not wait until the X an Y sperm are in the vagina before trying to separate them. A less complicated method would be to separate the X and Y sperm first and then use artificial insemination. As the X-carrying sperm are heavier than the Y this ought to be possible, and various ways of doing this have been tried, or are being developed, including filtration, electrophoresis and centrifugation. Despite such attempts, no reliable method of sex predetermination is currently available.

Until such time as an efficient and widely acceptable method of predetermining a child's sex before conception is available, the only way for a woman to ensure that she will give birth to a girl or a boy is if she knows the sex of the embryo or foetus beforehand. Methods of accurately determining the sex of the foetus do exist. Amniocentesis is a test which is usually used to detect foetal abnormalities, but can also reveal the sex of the foetus. The way this is done is to remove a small sample of the fluid surrounding the foetus and then carry out a chromosomal analysis of the cells contained in the amniotic fluid to determine whether there are XX or XY chromosomes present. Reliable and relatively safe though amniocentesis is, one of the major drawbacks to its use is that it can only be safely carried out at a relatively late stage of pregnancy, after the sixteenth week. This means that if the pregnancy is to be terminated on the grounds that the foetus is the 'wrong' sex, a late abortion would be necessary.

A newer technique known as chorionic villus sampling (CVS), whereby a small piece of the placenta is removed and analysed, can also detect the sex of the foetus and some foetal abnormalities. The advantage of this method is that it can be done as early as the eighth week; however the miscarriage rate is estimated to be slightly higher than with amniocentesis.

Another method of sex determination is to carry out genetic tests on embryos. Women who have IVF could have their embryos tested to find out whether XX or XY chromosomes were present and then only implant those of the desired sex, thus avoiding the possibility of a later abortion.

Sex selection in Britain is currently restricted to situations where there are good medical grounds for not wanting a boy or a girl. Under medical control, the present aim of such techniques is to screen for sex-linked diseases such as Duchenne muscular dystrophy and haemophilia. They are not used to enable people to choose the sex of their babies. Nevertheless, there have been cases reported of doctors carrying out gender abortions as a form of family planning.

In some other countries, for instance in parts of India, amniocentesis is offered to women as a sex determination test, along with abortion if the foetus is female. The tremendous pressure on Indian women to produce sons often means that a woman is in no position to resist this happening. A son brings status and wealth to a family, a daughter is more often seen as a liability. To stop the practice of female foeticide in India demands more than restrictions on the use of 'sex-choice' tests like amniocentesis. What is also needed is a fundamental change in the social and economic status of women (Kishwar, 1985).

If sex selection techniques were generally available in the West would people choose to use them? There is plenty of evidence that people do care a great deal about the sex of their children. The first question usually asked after a baby is born is whether it is a boy or a girl. That most people, men especially, prefer sons to daughters, particularly as first or only children, has also been well documented (for a discussion, see Corea *et al.*, 1985). If there was a willingness to use such methods, with such preferences what might the consequences be?

One suggestion is that family size might be reduced as people would not have to 'keep on trying' for a girl or a boy. Another suggestion is that the preference for sons would result in more boys and fewer girls being born, with people using sex-choice technology to make sure their first-born child was a boy. The presence of a much greater number of men than women is unlikely to threaten male supremacy. On the contrary, 'fewer women might mean greater pressure on women to marry and have children, thus reducing even further the control women have over their own bodies and their sexuality' (Hanmer, 1981).

From a feminist perspective this is a powerful argument for opposing the widespread use of sex-choice technology. However, if daughter preference could be strengthened feminist arguments against allowing people to choose the sex of their children would become rather less powerful. Sex-choice technology could help to achieve this, by enabling women to make a political choice to have only daughters and not sons. Not all feminists therefore would accept the view that sex-choice technology ought to be rejected totally. Some may have strong personal as well as political reasons for wanting sex-selection methods to become available, in terms of their own preferences for a daughter rather than a son. The important question for feminists who oppose such developments therefore is: Why shouldn't women have a right to choose only daughters?

Discussion of reproductive technology is not a new feminist concern. The issues of women's control over reproduction and motherhood have a long tradition within feminist politics. In the next chapter I will examine the history of this concern, and some of the questions and campaigns it has provoked.

6

Feminism and motherhood

What is meant by feminism has changed quite significantly in accordance with developments in thinking about how, and why, women are oppressed and, also, how gender relates to other forms of oppression, in particular 'race', class, sexuality, and age. Within contemporary feminist accounts it has been women's position within the home, especially as wives and mothers, which has generally been seen as the key to understanding women's oppression. But this has not always been the case. The idea that the sexual division of labour within the home needed to be challenged was absent from most early feminist writing. On the contrary, the belief that women should care for children and provide domestic services for men and dependent relatives is one which many feminists during the late nineteenth and the first half of this century appear to have accepted.

Equality in difference

During the nineteenth century feminism was mainly concerned with trying to improve the position of women outside the home. In challenging the idea of a natural separation of spheres of activity for women and men, a public sphere for men and a private sphere of the home and family for women, feminists of that era espoused the need for changes which would enable women to take a greater part in public life. They demanded, amongst other things, equal opportunities and rights for women with respect to education, employment and, of course, the vote.

Although it may have rejected certain aspects of the conventional female role, the nineteenth-century feminist movement largely accepted the idea that there were certain fundamental differences between the sexes, in particular that a maternal instinct existed in women and not in men. What they sought was equality in difference, believing that, though different, women should not be seen as subordinate to men. Specifically, they acknowledged the importance of motherhood and women's domestic role, trying to get domestic qualities to count for more in public life. It was argued that women had special talents and virtues which they developed in their role as wives and mothers, such as sympathy, caring and tenderness, and that it was desirable for women to extend these beyond the home. Paradoxically, then, underlying most nineteenth-century feminist arguments for women's greater participation in social and political life outside the home, was the belief that women were better suited by nature to domestic life than men. This, of course, was a belief which anti-feminists could also use to argue that a woman's place *was* in the home.

It is important to recognise that feminists then, as now, did not speak with one voice. There were some feminists who condemned the family as the source of women's inferiority and subordination. Theresa Billington-Greig, for example, writing in the early part of this century stated that 'any woman who is really a rebel longs to destroy the conventions which bind her in the home as much as those which bind her in the state'. Her proposed solution to this was to reject family life altogether, rather than to demand that its structure be altered. Along with a growing number of late nineteenth- and early twentieth-century feminists, she advocated spinsterhood as a deliberate choice, 'as the only means to intellectual fulfilment and a successful career' (Lewis, 1984, p. 89).

Health and welfare

The turn of the century brought an important change in social attitudes towards women's role as mothers. Prior to the twentieth century it was women's role as wife rather than mother which was stressed. From the beginning of the twentieth century, however, there is an increasing emphasis on the mother. Women, through their actual or potential maternity, were regarded as 'Saviours of the Race', engaged in the vitally important task of moulding the next generation on whom society's future hopes rested.

The appeal such developments held for many women in that era was the positive role and elevated status accorded motherhood. This was true for feminists also, many of whom continued to accept the view that women were better suited to work within the home than men. What was different about feminism after the turn of the century was an increasing emphasis on the welfare of mothers, on the very real problems and difficulties mothers faced, rather than the unique contribution women could make to public life by virtue of their special 'domestic' qualities. Unlike nineteenth-century feminism, the primary concern was trying to bring about changes which would improve the position of women within the home.

The Women's Co-operative Guild, for instance, campaigned to improve the maternity and infant welfare services available to poor women in Britain, for whom the expectation of death in childbirth remained quite high (and was to continue to do so up until the 1930s). As part of this campaign, the guild published a collection of letters from women members as evidence of the awful conditions in which many women had to give birth to and raise children (Llewelyn Davies, 1978).

After women had been granted the vote, the alliance between feminism and welfare increasingly dominated the British feminist movement. Campaigns continued to be directed at improving the conditions of mothers' lives, for example, through the introduction of family allowances and better health care for women and their children, including safer childbirth and access to birth control.

The latter was an important development within feminism. Feminists during the nineteenth and early part of the twentieth centuries did not believe that women should be mothers against their wills. They argued for 'voluntary motherhood', the right of women to refuse intercourse with their husbands if they did not wish to conceive (Gordon and Du-Bois, 1987). To achieve this feminists called for either complete chastity (hence the slogan Votes for Women, Chastity for Men) or for periods of abstinence and the exercise of male constraint. Few demanded a wider knowledge of birth control and the availability of contraceptives. On the contrary, far from seeing contraception as a step towards women's emancipation, many feminists regarded it as a means whereby men could indulge their sexual desires both within and outside marriage. By opposing birth control, they were concerned to protect women from the unwanted sexual demands of men and the possible consequences of an increase in extra-marital sex, in particular the risk of transmission of venereal disease and the loss of financial and emotional security if the marriage broke up (Jeffreys, 1985).

By contrast, support for contraception as a form of birth control emerged as a major issue within feminism during the twenties and thirties. This should not be interpreted as necessarily indicating that feminists' attitudes towards sexuality underwent a significant change during this period, although there was a greater insistence on the importance of sexual pleasure for women. The way in which this new interest in birth control was usually expressed was less in terms of sexual freedom for women, than with reference to the risks to women's health of excessive pregnancies and large families. By enabling women to space their pregnancies, it could be argued that both natural and artificial methods of birth control would lead to fewer, but more healthy babies being born to healthier mothers. In this sense birth control arguments, feminist or otherwise, could be used to sustain women's traditional role in the family, in terms of freeing her to perform better her maternal duties.

It was health concerns that were used to justify the limited though important change in government thinking on contraception in 1930. Prior to this, none of the major political parties in Britain had been willing to commit themselves to policies dealing with birth control. However by the beginning of the thirties the then Labour government accepted the need for the existing Maternity and Child Welfare Centres to give contraceptive advice to married women 'in cases where further pregnancy would be detrimental to health' (Weeks, 1990, p. 193).

The Abortion Law Reform Association, founded in 1936, also argued for reform primarily on health grounds. They claimed that if legal abortion were to be made available there would be a reduction in maternal deaths. Unlike the birth control campaigners, however, they made little progress until the sixties, when the 1967 Abortion Act was finally passed.

The continued concern within feminism for the welfare of mothers and their children coincided, in the forties, with the post-war emphasis on the importance of the mother and the need to relieve the burdens upon her. To some extent this may sound as if the British government was at last taking seriously what various women's organizations had been campaigning about for decades. However, fuelled by anxieties about what was considered to be a dangerously low birth-rate, the post-war government's concern with the protection of motherhood was, in reality, more about population control than women's welfare.

The response of feminists to this was diverse. There was no coherent feminist movement as such, nor had there been since the late twenties (Banks, 1981). Instead there existed a number of different women's groups and organizations who were, in some way or another, concerned with seeking equality with men. On the whole most of these did not oppose the post-war emphasis on women as mothers. Instead they regarded it as something which they could use to further their own political ends. For example, the response of women's labour organizations to this emphasis on motherhood was to object to it in so far as it took the form of criticisms of women going out to work, but to use it to argue for what they had long been fighting for, improved conditions for working class mothers (Riley, 1983a).

In the context of the post-war concern over the birth-rate, women's organizations were also able to argue that with improved access to birth control, many women would not choose to have larger families unless their working conditions were improved. They wanted the government to increase children's allowances, to provide better housing and nursery schools to relieve the stress and strain on tired mothers, and to allow access to such labour-saving devices as electric washing machines. Yet for all its talk about the importance of protecting the mother, the government actually did very little to provide services which would have made motherhood easier for women.

In their concern with improving conditions for mothers and their children, women's organizations during the post-war years accepted many of the traditional assumptions about the family and motherhood. Their aim was to make work within the home less tiring and stressful, not to challenge the fact that it was women who were primarily responsible for the care of the home and children. This was to change in the late sixties with the emergence of a new style of feminism, the women's liberation movement.

Women's liberation

Although it continued to argue the necessity of women's rights, the women's liberation movement went much further, and asked for far more, than had feminists of the inter-war period and the years after the Second World War. This new feminism offered 'a critique of women's traditional role that welfare feminism was not prepared to make' (Banks, 1981, p. 178). Feminists had previously challenged the conditions in which childcare and housework were carried out, as well as arguing for the wider social recognition of 'domestic qualities and duties'. But very few had ever questioned that this was women's work. Now feminists challenged this assumption, claiming that it was precisely women's traditional role within the home that was the key to understanding women's subordination.

Many of the feminist critiques of the family to emerge in the sixties were founded on women's own reported experiences of motherhood. In Britain there was the work of Hannah Gavron (1966), and in the United States Betty Friedan's earlier book, *The Feminine Mystique* (1963), publicised the frustration and isolation experienced by many predominantly white, middle-class mothers caring for small children. This concern with motherhood was no accident. It arose out of the changes that were taking place, by the late 50s and 60s, in the conditions of women's lives. At that time many women were facing contradictions and problems in trying to combine motherhood and paid employment or, alternatively, were feeling isolated in the home, caring for their children all day. These are concerns which still occupy women, and criticism of the heterosexual nuclear family, in which the responsibility for housework and childcare is assumed to be the woman's, remains central to feminist theory and practice in the nineties.

Feminist writers have attempted to research the experience of motherhood and childrearing in a variety of ways. They have, for example, described and analysed the experience of childbirth (Oakley, 1979 and 1980), the transition to motherhood (Breen, 1975), the lifestyles of mothers (Boulton, 1983), the processes through which mothering is reproduced (Chodorow, 1978), mother–daughter relationships (Arcana, 1981) and feminist mothers (Gordon, 1990), and challenged the myth of the maternal instinct (Badinter, 1981). Initially, however, feminist critiques of the family focused on the way in which beliefs about motherhood and the family were oppressive to women, in conditioning and constraining the views women held about themselves and their lives. What this meant in practice was that women were encouraged to examine, both individually and in consciousness-raising groups, the beliefs they had internalized about motherhood. Bowlby's theory of maternal deprivation was frequently held up for criticism by feminists, who rejected the idea of a maternal instinct to have children and to know how to care for them. Other writers drew attention to the idealization of motherhood as potentially problematic for women.

Looking back one can see why it may have seemed to some that feminists were against mothers and motherhood. Feminists in the early seventies tended to stress 'the isolation, conflict and economic dependence most women faced as full-time mothers or else the weary exhaustion of working mothers' (Segal, 1987). What this represented in part was a reaction to the idealized mother of the fifties, viewed as if through rose-tinted spectacles. From this perspective, it is understandable that many feminists felt it necessary to draw attention to the negative aspects of motherhood, and the campaigns of the women's liberation movement reflected this: better childcare provision and control over reproduction were among the first demands.

Childcare

Feminism during the sixties and early seventies was not solely confined to analysing how women experienced their own personal lives, in particular the complexities and contradictions of being a mother. Indeed one of the most important issues in the early years of the women's liberation movement was women's right to work on equal terms with men, for equal pay. It was argued, and still is by most feminists, that gender equality is ultimately dependent on women being able to participate on equal terms with men in paid employment outside the home. However for this ever to become a reality women first had to be relieved of their traditional responsibility for looking after children and the home. To this end, feminists pursued a variety of strategies for better childcare provision. One of the four basic demands agreed upon at the first

British women's liberation conference in Oxford in 1970 was free 24-hour nursery provision. (Equal pay, improved education and free contraception and abortion on demand were the others.) It was also suggested that men should take an equal share in childcare and housework.

Using a psychoanalytic framework, Nancy Chodorow some years later claimed that it is the fact that it is women and not men who mother which maintains women's subordination (Chodorow, 1978). Chodorow explains this in terms of the different dynamics of the mother–son and mother–daughter relationship. Her argument is that the identification of girls with their mothers prepares them for motherhood in a way that the early socialization of boys does not. In her view the fact that infants are usually cared for by women not only creates in girls a desire to have children, but also leads to their being better able and more willing to care for them than men. Chodorow thus relates women's oppression to the current division of childcare, which she sees as being based on psychological differences between women and men arising out of that division. For Chodorow, then, women's mothering is in some sense both natural and inevitable, given the dominant social structures and the current sexual division of labour. To break this self-perpetuating cycle, she suggests that men be persuaded to participate more equally with women in looking after children. Hopefully, this would lead to changes in the psychological development of girls and boys and to gender equality.

Many radical feminists would argue differently. They would claim that the reason men do not share childcare is because they do not want to, not because they are incapable. It is to their advantage that women do most of the housework and the work involved in looking after children. Another criticism that has been levelled at Chodorow's work is that it suggests all we need is a change in men's personalities. She does not explore the social and economic, as well as the psychological, changes that are necessary to make shared parenting more of a reality (see Chapter 1). Leaving aside any criticisms one might want to make of psychoanalytic approaches in general, such an analysis also implies a certain psychological, if not social, determinism in its emphasis on early childhood experiences as formative. Arguably, adult socialization is also important in the maintenance of gender divisions and certainly, from a feminist perspective, we should be wary of explanations which allow individual men to argue that they are what they are and cannot change. Indeed, as Lynne Segal has pointed out in her discussion of Chodorow's work, there is a tendency to ignore the fact that it is not necessarily men's personalities that remain stable, but the power relations which privilege male over female (Segal, 1987).

Another problem with the demand for men to take equal responsibility for the care of children is that it is of no use to women without a male partner (or co-parent) and women who do not want one. Related to this theme, there is also a danger that such a demand, baldly stated, could work against the struggle for better public provision of childcare generally. This is because the concept of 'shared parenting' does not appear to challenge the view that childcare is a private and personal responsibility.

Reproduction

It is women's capacity to reproduce or, more accurately, how this is defined and controlled, which is seen by many feminists to be at the heart of women's oppression (Graham, 1982). Juliet Mitchell, in her book *Women's Estate*, identified reproduction as one of her four structures of women's oppression, the others being production, sexuality and the socialization of children (Mitchell, 1971). Looking at reproduction as one aspect of women's oppression, Mitchell claimed that it is no use just trying to change this, as any modification in one of the four structures is likely to be offset by a reinforcement in another. For example, she observes that the twentieth-century decline in the importance of the reproduction of children has been accompanied by an increasing importance placed on the mother's role in childrearing.

Shulamith Firestone went further than this. She argued that women's oppression is a direct consequence of the fact that women, and not men, bear children (Firestone, 1971). Only by freeing women from the reproductive processes of pregnancy and childbirth, claimed Firestone, would women ever achieve social and economic equality with men. The key to women's liberation was artificial reproduction. However, as her critics have rightly pointed out, artificial reproduction could lead to a continuation or, possibly, an increase in male domination if women were not able to control the manner in which it was used. Having said that, the themes which Firestone and others explored, the relationship between women's oppression and reproductive science and technology, were important, and they retain their importance in the nineties as feminists debate the effects of new reproductive technologies. (This and other issues concerning Firestone's work are discussed in more detail in the previous chapter.)

While feminists like Firestone wanted to free women from reproduction there has since developed a strand of radical feminism, sometimes referred to as cultural feminism, which seeks to celebrate what are regarded as undervalued female attributes and female biology. Adrienne Rich was one of the first radical feminists to challenge Firestone's position of seeing women's biology as inherently oppressive. In her book *Of Women Born*, published in 1976, she explores the idea of female biology, in particular the potential to reproduce, as a source of power. Rich exercised caution in claiming special strengths for women; others have perhaps more clearly expressed the view that nature has endowed women with certain qualities which should be valued equally with, if not more than, those characteristics which are, supposedly, specific to men. Susan Griffin, for instance, appears to regard women as more nurturing by nature (Griffin, 1981), and in her work Mary Daly seems to be suggesting that there are inherent differences between women and men, including the possibility that men may be naturally more violent than women (Daly, 1979 and 1984).

Feminism's influence

Is the feminist movement right to attack the family? Some no longer think so. Though they may have once located women's oppression in their traditional role in the family, writers like Germaine Greer (1984) and Betty Friedan (1981) have revised their views and now argue in support of the family. For many feminists, however, the question of whether feminism was, and is, right to attack traditional ideas about women's place in the home is a practical one: how far does criticising the family limit how effective and widespread feminist challenges can be?

The enormous social pressures on women to get married and

have children in conjunction with, very often, a lack of any acceptable alternative, ensures that a high proportion of women continue to identify strongly with their traditional role within the home. There are also issues of 'race' to consider. Black feminists have been critical of white feminists' preoccupation with the family as crucial to understanding women's oppression for a number of reasons (hooks, 1982; Bhavnani and Coulson, 1986). For example, the white feminist critique of the family is likely to conflict both with Black women's view of the family as potentially supportive in a racist society, and with their need to defend their families against racist immigration procedures which may work to split them up. What this highlights is not only that Black and white women's experiences of the family are unlikely to be the same, but also that the experience of family life can be contradictory. As Stevi Jackson states, 'Patriarchal family structures may be oppressive for white *and* Black women, but families may also supply women with their closest and most supportive relationships, not least in relationships between women kin' (Jackson, 1992, p. 179).

The above may help to explain resistance to feminism (from both Black and white women), which some women see as representing a criticism of them and what they may regard as their major purpose and contribution in life. This is reflected in the way feminists are often portrayed as women who are both anti-children and anti-mothers. For example, it is Ann Dally's belief that 'Running through the women's liberation movement has been a thread of hostility to mothers and babies' (Dally, 1982, p. 179).

Although there is, undeniably, a certain tension between, on the one hand, not appearing to be against motherhood and children and, on the other, articulating the problems women experience as mothers, Dally's remark is a misrepresentation and a misunderstanding of what the feminist movement has tried to do. The aim has been to try and change the conditions of motherhood which limit women's experiences and choices. Adrienne Rich makes this point very clearly in identifying two meanings of motherhood: the potential of women to bear and rear children, and the institution of motherhood which creates the prescriptions and the conditions in which women experience the former (Rich, 1977). It is the institution of motherhood which feminism has challenged, not mothers or mothering.

It is not what feminists have said so much as what they have failed to say that has attracted other critics. Sylvia Hewlett, for example, claims that feminism has failed in the West because it has not paid sufficient attention to women's experience as mothers (Hewlett, 1987). It is true that feminism has only recently begun to grapple with the full complexity of women's capacity for maternity, as evidenced by books like this, but to pronounce its failure as a consequence of this is surely a little premature.

The question of whether feminism has paid sufficient attention to motherhood as an important sphere of women's activity also arises in connection with reproduction. The main emphasis in feminism's concern with enabling women to achieve control over their own fertility has been that of limiting reproduction, not extending it to all women. This has meant campaigns aimed at establishing 'the right to choose' not to get pregnant or to give birth; that is, demands for access to effective and safe contraception and abortion for all those who might need it. Feminism has paid less attention to 'the right to choose' to have children; although, in recent years, developments in reproductive technology have stimulated this debate (see Chapter 5). Discussion of this issue has also been prompted by accusations of racism. When Black women have a history of being coerced into family-planning decisions or forced sterilization or abortion, an emphasis on abortion rights and access to contraception will appear racist. This has led to a shift away from specific campaigns for abortion rights to a broader campaign for reproductive rights for all women, which encompasses campaigns against forced sterilizations and abortions as well as the right to have children how and when we want.

Other critics have in the past accused feminists of devaluing the work that women do in the home as mothers. For example, according to Mia Kelmer Pringle, the late Director of the National Children's Bureau:

> The necessary and justified aim of the Women's Movement to raise the consciousness and sense of personal identity of women has to a very considerable extent led to a further devaluing of mothering and to a misleadingly biased portrayal of young children. This is doubly unfortunate. It deprives many a young woman of a sense of joy and achievement when she creates a nurturing and happy environment for her family because she is made to feel that she is 'wasting' her abilities. And young babies are presented as mind-blowingly boring rather than

as engagingly individual, rapidly developing, though inevitably immature personalities. (Pilling and Pringle, 1978, p. 1)

Such conservative thinking blamed feminism for devaluing
motherhood. What it failed to recognize was that the feminist
challenge of the seventies emerged in response to the contradictions and problems women faced in the home, in particular
through being idealized as mothers. It is true that the women's
movement did acknowledge the second-rate status ascribed
women, did give voice to the negative aspects of running a home
and bringing up children, and did encourage women to question
their assumed role in society, but it did not necessarily deny the
pleasures of having and caring for children.

The latter has been more evident since the late seventies as,
increasingly, feminists began to reassess motherhood, paying more
attention to the pleasures as well as the problems associated with
having children. This trend was perhaps not unrelated to the
fact that many feminists who had been involved in the women's
liberation movement were, in their thirties, confronting the choice
of motherhood for themselves.

A political choice?

From the feminist movement's massive output of writing in the
last twenty years there have emerged a number of important
questions relating to motherhood. Should I or shouldn't I have
children? What are my feelings towards having a son or a daughter? How as a feminist do I bring up any children that I might
have? But it is the first of these – should I, shouldn't I? – which
is the most basic.

During the seventies feminist discussions of motherhood concentrated on the costs of women's lives of having children: the
restrictions that motherhood brought and the ambivalent and
often negative reactions women experienced in their role as
mothers. Writers such as Betty Friedan, Jessie Bernard, Kate
Millett, Adrienne Rich and other feminist theorists and
researchers challenged the myth of motherhood as all-fulfilling,
and attempted to describe and analyse the experience of motherhood as women felt and knew it. Given the emphasis on mother-

hood as problematic, it was not surprising that some women began to question whether they wanted to have children. To talk about choice was new, to suggest that one might positively decide not to have children was, at that time, radical. What is more, such talk was occurring at a time when women were beginning to have more choice about becoming mothers because of the development of the contraceptive pill. The choice not to have children represented for many women a political decision: it was a rejection of the traditional expectations of women to become mothers. In this context many feminists decided not to have children because they felt that motherhood, under current conditions, was incompatible with their political work as feminists, not least in terms of the impact it would have on their energy and independence.

This trend did not disappear during the eighties and feminists continued to campaign for improved conditions for mothers. Nevertheless, other feminist writing on motherhood emerged which began to discuss the positive side of having children and how motherhood could be a site of power for women. For some women this shift within feminism led to shifts in their own decisions about having children. That there had been a change of emphasis was also evidenced by feelings of regret or anger expressed by some feminists, that now they were too old to have children the women's movement had 'reclaimed' motherhood. Another significant change was the increased public awareness of lesbian mothers. For lesbian feminists the decision to have a child is a political choice, in so far as it is an assertion of a 'choice' which society tries to deny them.

Do women have to choose between feminism and having children? There are many ways of putting our feminist politics into practice. Some women, seeing how other women's lives have been affected by having children, may decide not to become a mother. Others feel there is important work to be done in raising children and that they can further feminism through the influence they can exert as feminist mothers (Gordon, 1989). The answer to the question then is that it will depend on how you view the problem and what your feminist politics are. If, like Shulamith Firestone, you regard women's oppression as a direct consequence of the fact that women bear children, then it seems likely that you will regard being a feminist and being a mother as incompatible. If, on the other hand, you do not accept that it is giving birth to children which is oppressive, but rather the conditions in which motherhood is experienced, then this need not be the case. From the latter perspective the aim of feminism is not to free women from motherhood but from the conditions in which they find motherhood oppressive. For some women present conditions make motherhood an unacceptable 'choice'. Others, because they regard these conditions as unlikely to change in the near future and because they have a strong desire to have children, are willing to struggle with the contradictions and conflicts of being a feminist mother. The next chapter examines some of these contradictions and conflicts.

7

Feminism and childrearing

In the early seventies feminists claimed that women and men had been conditioned to feel and act differently. Women's liberation involved becoming aware, through consciousness-raising, of how we had been conditioned. This emphasis on the power of conditioning also suggested a way of bringing about social change through non-sexist childrearing.

Feminists who remain committed to the goal of trying to bring up children in a less sexist way are more likely to refer to this, in the nineties, as anti-sexist childrearing. This suggests a more active challenging of gender divisions than does the more neutral term, non-sexist childrearing. These two approaches share a common view, but there are differences in emphasis as to how to challenge the situation. Non-sexist childrearing sees the way that girls are socialized as a problem; the aim is to give girls an upbringing where they can have equal access to experiences and situations in order to be able to do things traditionally dominated by boys/ men, if they so choose. One of the dangers of this perspective is that it implies access is all that matters, allowing some to argue that if women are given equal access and do not enter certain areas of employment or achieve certain positions in society then it must be their own choice/fault. Anti-sexist childrearing differs from this basically equal-opportunities perspective, in seeing the problem as being much more than simply making sure that girls have access to what boys are allowed and encouraged to do. It is also concerned with the power relations which structure the way girls are treated and affect the outcome of girls' experiences. From an anti-sexist perspective it is male power and privilege that is the problem, not just girls' limited access to certain types of experience.

These two perspectives are not opposing viewpoints, and at the individual level women may adopt one or other position depending on the context. Whether they refer to it as anti-sexist or non-sexist childrearing, feminists share the belief that it is in the best interests of the child, but more especially girls, to raise them to question and criticise stereotyped views about what women and men, girls and boys, are like. That is the aim; how does this manifest itself in practice?

What is anti-sexist childrearing?

Is anti-sexist childrearing encouraging girls to play with train-sets and boys to play with dolls; challenging sexist messages in books and on television; rewarding girls for being confident and adventurous and boys for being gentle and sensitive; avoiding reinforcing what are traditionally thought of as 'masculine' and 'feminine' characteristics and behaviour?

Very little has so far been written on what anti-sexist or non-sexist childrearing might involve outside a school setting (Carmichael, 1977; Grabucker, 1988). One possible interpretation would be to attempt to treat girls and boys exactly the same. The problem with this is that there are many other influences on children's ideas besides those of parents. Toy manufacturers, books, television programmes, and adverts very often present children with a highly stereotyped view of what women and men are like. Teachers, peers and relatives may also encourage traditional interests and activities. Anti-sexist childrearing could therefore also be taken to mean treating girls and boys quite differently in an attempt to redress the balance. As one woman commented:

> I noticed when I said my daughter was aggressive I would perhaps have attempted to tone down the aggression in the boys, whereas I'm pleased to see it in her. I tend to let her do things that are a bit wild. I might have said to the boys watch this, or careful, but I deliberately don't say that to her in case she thinks I'm saying careful because she's a girl.

For the parents in one study non-sexist childrearing meant

'opening up options' for their children, rather than preventing them from doing certain things (Statham, 1986). These parents did not see themselves as trying to reverse roles, but as encouraging children to feel they had a choice and that they did not need to feel they could not do a whole range of things just by virtue of being female or male. It is interesting to note, particularly as concepts of sexuality are fundamental to the construction of power relations between women and men, that this desire to 'open up options' for their child did not extend to considering alternatives to heterosexuality.

Challenging traditional beliefs and expectations about women and men, girls and boys, is an important aspect of anti- and non-sexist childrearing. It is equally important that children are made aware of the social forces operating which maintain the differences in power and opportunities between women and men, and constrain our choices. The parents in June Statham's study wanted their children to understand what sexism meant. They also wanted to foster qualities, such as self-confidence and independence, which would help the children to stand up for their beliefs, regardless of social pressure (Statham, 1986).

Children do not start out from equal positions of power, but are divided by class, 'race' and gender. Although the general aim of an anti-sexist upbringing is to enable the child to recognize and challenge male supremacy, this will take different forms, as well as having different consequences, for girls and for boys. With girls one is primarily concerned with helping them to develop skills to enable them to challenge and resist sexism in others, as well as giving them a positive opinion of themselves and what they can do. For boys it involves learning that girls are their equals and that it is incorrect and unfair to believe men are superior.

Because this means relinquishing power and privilege, many boys are likely to resist and resent such efforts. There may be problems in getting them to see 'what's in it for them' – something parents are likely to have a much easier time convincing girls of! This is one of the reasons why anti- or non-sexist childrearing is often regarded as more difficult, if not impossible, with a boy than with a girl. Another is the uncertainty over how to bring up a non-sexist boy. With girls the goals may seem much clearer: to open up opportunities and positively encourage non-traditional interests. With boys, encouraging non-traditional behaviour may stir up fears about homosexuality or rejection from peers for being a 'sissy'.

Some of these issues are discussed in more detail later on. But first let us consider the different dynamics operating between mothers and daughters and mothers and sons.

Mothers and daughters

The dominant discourse has been that of psychologists and psychiatrists, who claim that it is primarily through identifying with and imitating our mothers that we learn, as girls, to become feminine (or not) and heterosexual (or not). For example, lesbianism has been seen to result from a girl becoming fixated on her mother, failing to reject her mother as a love object, and identifying with her mother's lesbianism. Elsewhere I have discussed some of the reasons why such 'explanations' of lesbianism are invalid and, more generally, why the concept of identification with a parent of the same sex is far too simplistic a model to account for the way in which our sexualities, and our beliefs about gender, are constructed (Richardson, 1981b). Here I merely wish to draw attention to the fact that it is commonly assumed that the identities of mother and daughter are, in an important sense, inter-related.

How does this compare with women's own experiences as mothers and daughters? Various feminist writers have attempted to analyse their own and other women's experiences as daughters and mothers (Arcana, 1981; Park and Heaton, 1987). For example, Nancy Friday, analysing her relationship with her own mother, claimed that the way in which we see ourselves as women is intimately connected to how we perceive our mothers (Friday, 1979). Whilst this may not ring true for all women, for many – myself included – there is at least the feeling that a great deal of what was initially learnt about what it means to be 'a woman' was through relating to our mothers. This is not to say that such relationships are inevitably determining, and that we cannot change as a result of experiencing them, only that the relationship a girl has with her mother can be important in the construction of herself as a woman. This is no less true of the woman who says to herself, 'I don't ever want to become like my mother', or for whom an important aspect of her self-identity is never having had a mother. In each of these cases there is a part of self that is defined in relation to a mother figure.

This is not to ignore the powerful influence, both positive and negative, which fathers can have on their daughters' lives. However in a society divided by gender, the mother–daughter relationship will be marked by the fact that, as two women, there is far greater potential for each to identify with the other's position. For example, my early feelings about not wanting to get married or have children revolved primarily around my understandings of the lives of my mother and her friends, not my father and his. Similarly, becoming a mother is often a time when a woman may feel she now understands much more about her own mother, and how it felt to be her daughter, than she does about her father and the relationship she has had with him.

By the same token a woman may seek in her daughter an extension of herself. This may be one of the reasons that she wants a daughter. I am aware that my own desire, if I had a child, to have a daughter and not a son is partly linked to the greater expectation I have of a shared relationship being possible with a daughter. This is a feeling which I believe cannot entirely be put down to my feminism, for there are many women who are not feminists who also have this expectation. What this can mean is that the role of daughter carries with it certain expectations that the role of son does not. Although many women are sufficiently satisfied with their own lives not to seek a vicarious existence through a daughter, there are some who expect their daughters to provide them with purpose and meaning. A common way of expressing this is to put pressure on a daughter to get married and have a child. This can be implicit, perhaps by the mother not valuing what her daughter does – her work or her sexuality, for example – because this appears to make motherhood unlikely. It can also be explicit, for example, by continually asking 'when are you going to start a family?' As a man, who is not expected to become a father in the same way that women are expected to become mothers, a son can more easily escape such pressures.

Women who are dependent on their daughters for a sense of self and purpose may fiercely resist that which seems likely to prevent this. In the *Unlit Lamp* (1981), for example, Radclyffe Hall brilliantly evokes such possibilities in describing the relationship of Joan Ogden and her mother Mary who, in the name of love, thwarts her daughter's every attempt to leave her and the seaside town where they have always lived. Whether it is as a loving or as a hostile mother that women convey such expectations to their daughters, it can lead to daughters feeling that they will never become independent of their mothers or guilty if they do so.

Sons are rarely made to feel guilty for wanting to become independent of their mothers. On the contrary, it is regarded as an important part of a boy's growing up and becoming 'a man', that he breaks free from his mother's apron strings. Mothers know this and very often accept it, either because they feel this to be right or because they recognize that their struggle against their sons' desire for masculinity and male approval is one which they could never win (Rich, 1977). Traditional expectations of women and men may also help to explain why a mother may feel a certain amount of competition, or even in some cases resentment, over a daughter enjoying opportunities that were denied to her more than she would if a son, who is expected to achieve, were doing so.

In addition to those mothers who are envious of their daughters' apparent freedoms, or blame them for not being dutiful daughters, there is also the possibility that mothers will feel guilty towards their daughters. Informed by theories which tell us that daughters model themselves on their mothers in a way that sons do not, a mother may feel that how her daughter has turned out is largely a reflection of her. Obviously this can be a source of satisfaction and pleasure, but it can also lead to mothers feeling guilty if they perceive their daughters as unhappy, odd or 'deviant'. For example, one of the problems lesbians have in telling their mothers that they are a lesbian is that the latter may assume that this is somehow about them – their 'fault'. Typically this leads to the daughter being blamed by the mother, who at the same time feels guilty for causing what she does not want to accept in her daughter.

Many good mother–daughter relationships exist, despite these pressures. Others suffer from the expectations attached to being a 'good mother' or a 'dutiful daughter'. As I have already suggested, daughters sometimes blame their mothers for not being the mother they wanted and mothers may blame their daughters for not giving them what they expected from a daughter. This can lead to both feeling inadequate and that it is they who are somehow at fault. Whilst these are powerful feelings, they derive from stereo-typic expectations and myths of motherhood/daughterhood; it is these which are at fault. Feminism has played an important role in challenging and transforming such constructions, but this is not an easy task. There is still a great deal to be understood about the way we construct our identities as mothers and daughters, a process that is embedded in assumptions and expectations about women (in particular the development of femininity and sexual identities), mothers and children.

The question of sons

The recognition that, in a society where men have certain powers and privileges over women, our sons could one day be our oppressors can make mothering a male child seem problematic. This process can begin early. It is distressing to watch the develop-ment of behaviours and attitudes which are contemptuous of women in a male child whom one loves, for example, a boy who says to his sister or his female playmates, 'You're only a girl!' It may even be apparent right from birth, in terms of the greater value that is frequently placed on a woman having a son rather than a daughter.

Some women feel very strongly that they would not want a son and try to maximize their chances of conceiving a girl, for example by following a special diet or carefully timing when they conceive (see p. 106). For others the strength of their preference for a daughter can be gauged by their reactions to giving birth to a son. Apart from disappointment, a woman may experience feelings of failure, guilt or anger at discovering that 'It's a boy!' (Arcana, 1983). Women who feel like this are often castigated for their gender preference. Yet in many parts of the world such feelings have been accepted for generations as understandable responses to having a girl, especially as a first-born child.

A woman who gives birth to a male child knows that as he grows older he will be expected to reject or deny his attachment to her, and her influence over him, in order that he may be accepted into 'a man's world'. It is primarily to gain the acceptance and approval of other men, and the power that is associated with this, that a son does not want to be identified as a 'mummy's boy'.

Knowing this, and knowing also that they are expected to facilitate this process, mothers can become involved in painful contradictions with their sons. Aware of the lure of male approval, some women are concerned that their struggle to bring up boys to be non-sexist is one they will not win. As a feminist mother analysing her relationship with her own son, Angela Hamblin acknowledges such conflicts, in particular that to succeed as a man her son 'will have to turn his back on me and everything I have tried to teach him since infancy' (Hamblin, 1982).

Some women also worry that, should this happen, they will be accused by their sons of having failed them and be rejected along with their feminist beliefs. These are fears which, Adrienne Rich claims, cannot be avoided. Women who want their sons to grow up to recognize and challenge sexism have to confront the fact that this may mean that their sons will feel very alone in the 'world of men' and may, as a result, come to hate them for this (Rich, 1977).

However angry and disappointed a woman may be at her son for having failed her, she may also experience a sense of guilt and loss in having failed him. Women who are raising their sons to challenge male privilege and the expression of 'masculinity' are frequently charged with damaging their sons. This is meant to provoke guilt and it is understandable when it does. The accusation 'bad mother' cuts deep, especially when it is backed up by social beliefs which idealize motherhood as self-sacrifice.

Another worry some women have, even if they are committed to bringing up a son to challenge male power and privilege, is that for a boy to become too attached to his mother could lead to him growing up to be gay. As I have explained elsewhere (Richardson, 1981b), we actually know very little about why men love and desire other men and even less about why some men and not others identify as heterosexual. This does not, however, prevent some people from assuming that male homosexuality is the result of a certain type of relationship between a mother and son. Nowhere is this more apparent than within psychoanalytic accounts of sexual development. In such a framework being homosexual is often understood in terms of unresolved Oedipal conflicts in early childhood, whereby the son is said to cope with feelings of hostility and aggression he has for his mother by identifying with her rather than with his father. This process is said to be most likely to occur when there is a weak or absent father, in conjunction with the son having a close and intimate relationship with a domineering and dominant mother. Such concepts filter through on a popular level, and are expressed in the fears some women have of being over protective or over intimate with their sons. For example, one woman said of her relationship with her four-month-old son:

> One thing I feel may be a problem is this mother's boy syndrome. I think it's acceptable for a mother to be very close to her daughter, not only emotionally, but to physically touch and fondle a little girl. . . . What is acceptable between mother and daughter may not be quite acceptable between mother and son, there may be sort of overtones of Oedipus and all that and the other. I think that could come into it at some stage a bit later on.

Even among those women who do not wish their sons to grow up to accept, unquestioningly, the expectation that they will be both 'masculine' and heterosexual, there very often exists the feeling of not wanting their child to be alienated from his friends through being labelled as different to other boys.

For some women bringing up a male child seems too contradictory an experience to go through given their political beliefs. For example, as a political strategy within radical feminism relationships with men can be seen as a drain on women's energy and as undermining feminist politics. For this reason some radical feminists would argue that successfully to challenge women's oppression women should, as far as possible, seek to exclude men from their lives. Consequently they may feel that, in the absence of an efficient method of sex selection being widely available, they would prefer not to have children at all rather than have to face the conflicts which they see raising a son as involving. Other women, however much they may prefer to have a daughter, are willing to take the risk that they may give birth to a male child.

What do feminists want for their sons? Women who have begun to challenge the way women are oppressed by men are, claims Adrienne Rich, 'haunted by this question' (Rich, 1977). They may know what it is they do not want their sons to be like, but are unclear about what to encourage them to be instead. If this is true, it may be partly because we lack a feminist analysis of children's needs and childrearing practices (Riley, 1983b). In the present climate, where the needs of children often contradict and conflict with women's demands for liberation, it may be politically inadvisable, or even impossible, to achieve such an analysis. There is, however, nothing intrinsically anti-feminist about a concern for children and, as many feminist mothers know only too well, there are certain questions which we need to address. Are there, for instance, distinct feminist objectives in the care of children and, if there are, what would a feminist understanding and approach to childrearing be?

Parents as role-models

One way a child learns about gender is through the experience of being treated differently by parents and other adults. Certain types of behaviour are encouraged and other discouraged in girls but not in boys, and vice versa, in accordance with what is and is not considered appropriate for one's gender. Direct reinforcement of what a child says or does cannot, however, fully explain how children learn what women and men are expected to be like. Children may also be influenced in their ideas about gender through observing other people and modelling their behaviour on them.

Some researchers regard the process of learning about gender as considerably more complex than this. The cognitive developmental approach, for example, sees children as actively structuring their understanding of gender roles, rather than passively learning them through reinforcement and modelling. It is argued that all children will go through a stage of wanting to conform to stereotyped expectations of what girls and boys are like, irrespective of what their parents or teachers may say or do. Once they become aware they are a girl or a boy, around the age of two to three, they seek out opportunities to behave in ways which they see as being 'female' or 'male'. According to cognitive developmental theory, this is because at this age the child's understanding of what it means to be a girl or a boy is very restricted. Doing what girls or boys are expected to do is what being a girl or being a boy actually means. You are a girl because you play with dolls. You are a boy because you wear trousers and not a dress. As children develop cognitively they will be increasingly capable of understanding that you remain a girl or a boy, woman or man, even if you do not do the things that girls or boys are traditionally expected to. They become aware, in other words, that masculinity and femininity are not absolute but relative concepts, whose meaning can vary. Despite important theoretical differences between cognitive developmental, psychoanalytic and social learning theory approaches, what is common to most theories of gender-role development is the concept of identification with a parent of the same gender. Although there are variations in how the term identification is used, generally speaking it refers to the child's desire to be like the parent not only by imitating what they do, but also by incorporating what the child perceives are their values and beliefs. The concepts of reinforcement, modelling and identi-fication have been critically discussed elsewhere (see, for example, Richardson, 1981b). What is primarily of interest here are the implications for non-sexist childraising, in particular the emphasis on parents as role-models for their children.

Informed by such theories, it is hardly surprising that many parents who want to bring up their child to be anti- or non-sexist think it important they avoid stereotypic roles. For example, one woman said she resisted the expectations of her as a mother, not only because she felt this to be necessary for herself but also because, as a role-model for her daughter, she wanted to demon-strate that such possibilities exist.

I want her to grow up realising I am not a provider for her every whim, whose thoughts, interests, and actions are all done with her. I want her to grow up realising I've got my own life to lead, that I have my own commitments that are entirely independent from her, without her feeling insecure or unwanted. I want her to understand that as much for her own sake as mine.

Another woman was concerned about the influence that her not going out to work could have on her son.

I think if I don't do something then he might say, 'well, look I had a mother who was involved in the women's liberation movement and yet look what she did, she stayed at home.' So I think that in a way it's up to me to do something, to show him that a woman can contribute as much to society as a man. . . . I should think that would be the biggest influence as much as anything.

Equally, a woman may be concerned about who looks after her child if she does go out to work. For example, the following woman no longer felt able to leave her daughter with the childminder who had looked after her during her first year because:

> I could see she would say things to Louise and ask her to do things that I really wouldn't agree with. She would want to superimpose on Louise the conventional little girl.

Whilst acknowledging that both girls and boys are likely to learn a great deal about gender through their observations in the home, the responsibility for this need not only rest with the mother. For women in heterosexual relationships it will also depend on how their male partner behaves. What example does he set? Does he, for instance, share responsibility for household jobs such as washing, cooking and cleaning? Is he equally involved in childcare?

Sharing paid employment, housework and childcare more equally between women and men is an important part of many people's view of non-sexist childrearing. Most of the parents in June Statham's study said they had attempted to do this. They felt that in this way they could set an example for their children by showing them men doing housework and looking after children and women working outside the home. However in practice there were important limits to the extent to which fathers were involved in childcare. In most families it was the woman who was mainly responsible for this (Statham, 1986).

One explanation for this is men's attitudes: men do not share responsibility for housework or rearing children because they choose not to. This is undoubtedly often true, but it is also the case that choices are constrained by social and economic factors. The unequal employment opportunities for women, the scarcity of day-care, the low pay and low status of part-time work, the relationship between masculinity, male self-esteem and paid work, as well as the existence of few opportunities for job-sharing, limit the possibilities for women and men to share childcare and paid employment. Clearly wider changes in the way that society is structured to men's advantage are going to be needed, if non-sexist childraising is to be more than liberal idealism.

School

However much a parent might be able to exercise control over the influences on a child during her early years, this will become increasingly difficult once the child goes to school. Despite attempts in recent years to develop equal opportunities and anti-sexist approaches, there are many aspects of school life which continue to reinforce traditional beliefs about what women and men, girls and boys, are like. Observational studies have shown how teachers, both blatantly and in subtle ways, very often treat girls and boys differently. Most schools divide children by gender whether it is in lining them up, listing them separately on the register, or segregating them for certain subjects on the basis of expected interests, for example, restricting football to boys and childcare to girls (Whyld, 1983).

There are other aspects of school life which reinforce the impression that men are more important than women, Examination of the way women and men are represented within the curriculum, and in text books, indicates that most children encounter a male-dominated environment at school. Book lists are dominated by books written by men about men. Not only are women severely under-represented in most subjects, but when they are mentioned they are often depicted as inferior to men. The position of women and men in the staff hierarchy further reinforces notions of male supremacy. Women staff are generally paid less than men, and occupy fewer positions of authority within schools (Davidson, 1985).

What can parents do about sexism within schools? One possibility is to try to get the school to change its policies. Another strategy, given that this may be no easy task, is to try to counteract the school's influence by encouraging children to be critical of the stereotyping that goes on there. Alternatively, parents may try to find a school which seems to offer their child a less sexist education. For example, some parents would prefer their daughters went to a single-sex rather than a mixed-sex school, in the hope of reducing what they see as the negative influences of coeducation on girls.

I favour single sex schools, an aggressive girl – or what's called aggressive in a girl – there's more place for her than in a mixed school and, vice versa, the gentler boy in a boy's school. Also, in all-girls schools women are in the top jobs and have the power, which they *don't* in mixed schools. I think they take on the accepted roles more in a mixed-sex school.

Many parents share this woman's concern with coeducation, seeing it as effectively 'girls going into boys' schools' (Whyld, 1983). Contrary to what was expected, coeducation has not opened up educational opportunities for girls. Research studies have shown that although pupils are more likely to be offered non-traditional subjects in a mixed school, they are more likely to tackle them in a single-sex school (Mahoney, 1985). For example, girls are more likely to do maths and science in an all-girl than a coeducation school. They are also more likely to pursue further and higher education generally and experience women in positions of authority and power. However as far as achievement is concerned, studies of examination results show that girls and boys in single-sex schools perform very similarly to children in coeducation schools (Steedman 1983).

For many parents, however, the debate over the value of single-sex schooling is largely theoretical. Nowadays the choice of sending a girl to a single-sex school is restricted to those who can afford to pay for such an education, although some mixed schools, as part of anti-sexist teaching methods, do offer single-sex classes in certain subjects, maths for instance.

The question of whether mixed comprehensive schooling is equally beneficial to girls and boys in a social as well as an academic sense is also one that concerns some parents. A number of studies have identified how girls 'loose out' in the learning process through the sexual harassment they experience in mixed schools, which is largely unacknowledged and unchallenged (Lees, 1986; Halson, 1989). Carole Jones (1985) argues that this makes mixed schools dangerous for girls; they are places where boys practice and become skilled at exercising power over girls and women. The important aspect of single-sex schooling affecting the outcome of girls' educational experiences, from this perspective, is that they are not under the same pressures from their peers.

Peer pressure

One of the main influences on children is other children. Once a child has begun school friends become increasingly important in determining their ideas about what it means to be female or male. Very often, it seems, the peer group overwhelmingly reinforces traditional gender-role stereotypes. For instance, by seven years of age, and still more by eleven, there is a polarisation of interests, activities and playmates according to gender. It is the norm that girls play with girls and boys play with boys, both groups mutually scorning the other.

The pressure to conform to the values of one's peer group can be severe. If a boy deviates too far from what is expected of him as a male he runs the risk of being socially isolated and also of being labelled a 'sissy'. This may cause problems for parents as well as boys.

> There is a bit of conflict there for me, because there is this feeling . . . obviously you don't want him to be what people call a sissy, you don't want him when he's older to be regarded as that, but there again I don't feel he should be a stereotyped male in society. So I think there will be a conflict at some stage, both for him and for me.

For girls there is a corresponding risk that they may find it hard to make friends and be labelled a 'tomboy'. There are, however, differences in the extent to which girls and boys are pressurized into conforming to gender-roles. Tomboyish behaviour in girls, at least up until adolescence, carries less stigma than does so-called sissy behaviour in boys. It is, for example, viewed as more acceptable for a girl to want a football or a racing car, than it is for a boy to want a doll or a make-up kit. As a result, boys are more likely to be ridiculed by their peers for not conforming to the expectations of them as males, than are girls for being tomboys.

This can be partly explained in terms of the greater value and status attached to being male and masculine in our society. Also, a boy being labelled a sissy is likely to stir up fears about his sexuality in a way that calling a girl a tomboy does not. (A more comparable word might be butch, but this is usually applied to women and not girls.) Being a tomboy is usually seen as a relatively normal phase of development which many girls go through.

It would seem that parents who believe in the importance of

raising children to challenge gender divisions often do worry about what the consequences of peer pressure may be for their children, especially boys. Some of these worries are understandable enough. No one wants their child to be without friends, or to be teased or bullied for being different. But other worries, such as the belief that the child will grow up gay, have less foundation and are rooted in discrimination and prejudice.

Other influences

A girl has to learn to grow up into a person who will be discriminated against because she is not male. One important aspect of this learning is the kind of language she acquires. The development of feminist perspectives on language and its use have emphasised how language conveys meanings which both reflect, and help to maintain, women's oppressed position in society. In *Man Made Language*, for example, Dale Spender (1980) argued that language reflects male experience and perpetuates male power. Slag, bitch, dog, nag, tart are just a few of the long list of words that are often used to describe and condemn women – to keep them in their place. Other writers (for example, Rich, 1977; Daly, 1979) have experimented with ways of creating a language which reflects female experience and serves the interests of women. This struggle for the redefinition of the meanings of words and the value of meanings has continued and feminist critique of language has come a long way in the years since Dale Spender's book was published. Now it is a well-established subject in its own right. Feminist views on language are varied and complex, with contributions from a broad range of disciplines and theoretical perspectives. (For an overview of the way the feminist critique of language has developed, see Cameron, 1990).

Being aware of the role of language in communicating certain expectations about women and men can obviously affect how a person uses language. It may make some women particularly conscious of the way in which they, and other people, talk to their children.

Sometimes I find myself telling her she's pretty, because she is pretty, and I think 'Oh, maybe I shouldn't say that . . . Instead of pretty I might say something like, 'Oh, you're very good-looking or you're handsome, or you've got a nice face.' I don't want her to be the 'pretty little girl'.

This woman also felt that the kind of clothes a child is dressed in may affect the process of gender-stereotyping. Despite the move away from regulation pink and blue towards greater variety in children's wear, there continues to exist a differentiation between clothes for girls and clothes for boys. The style and colour of clothing, especially at the more physically ambiguous baby stage, is a way of emphasizing what gender a child is and can influence the way they are treated. For example, in a now-famous study a group of mothers were observed playing with a six-month-old child dressed in a frilly pink dress and called Beth. Their behaviour was compared to that of a different group of mothers who were observed playing with the same child, but this time dressed in blue rompers and given the name Adam. What the researchers found was that people react differently towards a child depending on whether they think it is a girl or a boy. Beth was offered a doll to play with more than Adam, who was more often given a train. It was also commented by some mothers that Beth was sweeter and cried more softly than a boy would. In fact, Beth was a boy (Will *et al.*, 1974).

This can happen in real-life as well as in experimental situations. One woman said this about her own three year old daughter:

> When she was little I always dressed her as a boy, firstly, well she always has hand-me-downs anyway and wore trousers, and then people used to behave towards her in quite a different way. If they can see it's a little girl they say [soft voice] 'Oh, a little girl,' and if it's a boy they say [gruff voice] 'Oh, he's a fine little fella isn't he'. It varied how people treated her according to what she was wearing.

Toys and games also offer a way of learning about the different beliefs and expectations held about girls and boys. As a visit to almost any toy shop will quickly reveal, many of the toys targeted at girls are domestic toys (miniature irons, microwaves, cookers, washing machines, etc.) or fashion accessories for themselves or their dolls. Toys aimed at boys are more likely to encourage mechanical or scientific skills, sports and outdoor activities, and war games.

Though they might make an exception if a child specifically asked for and very much wanted a particular toy, many people do still continue to buy what are generally thought of as boys' toys for a boy and girls' toys for a girl. For example, girls are not usually given boxing gloves or a gun, boys are not usually given miniature hoovers or a doll (unless it is dressed for armed combat).

Parents who are concerned about such stereotyping of children's interests and activities, can, instead, encourage girls and boys to play with a wide range of toys, not just those which are considered appropriate to their gender. What this often seems to mean in practice is providing girls with so-called boys' toys, and so-called girls' toys for a boy, in an attempt to balance out the toys which relatives and friends buy.

> I'd desperately avoid buying him a gun or any sort of war things, because I think they have enough of them to start. I don't think there's any need to encourage that sort of thing. It's the same as girls being given tea sets and nurses uniforms, if they want them fair enough, but so many other people will be buying things like that. I like to think that I could perhaps offer them something a bit different.

The kind of toys friends and relatives buy may reinforce traditional views about girls and boys. Should parents let their child keep toys which they themselves would not buy? Answers are likely to vary according to the kind of toy given and how important parents feel it is to prevent their child from playing with such a toy or game.

> It's difficult if it's given to the child because it's hard to take it away from them. If it's given to the parents they can choose to give it to the child or not. I'd probably try to take it away and put it somewhere he couldn't find it and see if he noticed it was missing.

However hard one might try to raise a child to challenge male supremacy, one's efforts will inevitably be undermined by other so[...]zation influences. For example, the view of the world [...]o children by books, comics, film and television is a highly [...] one. In most children's books the main characters are [...] men. When women do appear they are predominantly [...]s the weaker sex and/or in domestic roles. Television and film, with some rare exceptions, also continue to present children with an equally stereotyped view of what women and men can do.

It is difficult to say how far children are affected by these images, but even if they do not directly copy what they read in books or see on television it is likely that the images they receive will have an influence on how they think.

To counteract this, some parents and teachers make an effort to provide children with books which show women and men, girls and boys, involved in non-stereotyped activities and situations, an aim which has been made easier by the publication of specifically non-sexist books for children. Another strategy is to discuss the images presented in the media and story books, as a way of encouraging children to be critical of the messages they receive about girls and boys.

Given the reality of gender as a structuring element in society and in personal relationships, it would be impossible to raise a child without reference to their gender. What feminist movements want is an end to social and economic divisions on the basis of gender; an end to male supremacy. In this chapter I have discussed some of the problems of trying to translate this political aim into practice, by encouraging children to be conscious of the way male power and privilege operates in society.

8

Conclusion

As women we are socialized to believe that, within certain social contexts, having children and caring for them is both natural and necessary. One of the aims of this book has been to challenge those beliefs, which serve to limit women's experiences and choices with regard to having or not having children. It is not only through having more money that women will gain greater control over their own lives, but also through being able to say, 'I don't have to find a man; I don't have to get married; I don't have to have children'.

Apart from the social pressures which, to varying degrees, inform women that they ought to become mothers, the opportunities women have to control their own fertility will also be crucial to whether or not they have children. As I have indicated, despite the existence of highly reliable forms of birth control and the development of new reproductive technologies, women do not have reproductive freedom. A further aim of this book, therefore, has been to explore the forces shaping women's reproductive decisions. The importance of doing this is clear when women's reproductive 'rights' are increasingly coming under attack.

Just as there are many different reasons why women do or do not have children, so too there are many different meanings associated with becoming and being a mother. As I have illus-
t~ motherhood is not a universal experience; rather, it
on the particular conditions – both social and economic
~ individual women give birth to and rear children. For
~ving the help and support of a partner, family and
~ving enough money to be able to pay for someone

to look after one's child, are things that are likely to make a significant difference to how a woman experiences motherhood. What changes should be made to make life easier for women as mothers? To begin with women should not have to perceive having a child and having a job as alternatives. Or, if they do take paid employment, women should not have to choose work which conflicts least with being a mother or end up worn out trying to combine work and childcare responsibilities. As long as women and not men are penalized in this way for having children women will continue to suffer the negative effects of being financially dependent on men or on state benefits. Most feminists would associate the powerlessness of women in society with women's lack of financial independence, and would further believe that women will only gain such independence when they are able to participate on equal terms with men in paid employment. To do this we must seek to remove the many discouragements to women with young children undertaking paid work. A particular problem is the acute shortage of day-care facilities, coupled with a system of beliefs which informs women that they should be the ones who are responsible for the care of their child, and that going out to work will be detrimental and damaging to their relationship with their child.

Although it is important to seek support for those who care for children by demanding, amongst other things, improved child benefits, day-care facilities and the provision of crèches in public buildings, we must be careful not to fall into the trap of identifying such concerns as inherently and necessarily those of women. This would leave women in the position still, of being seen as having primary responsibility for childcare. If motherhood is to become a less exhausting, onerous and costly experience for women the work and the responsibility of childcare needs to be shared. The question is, with whom?

As we have seen, at present men make only the barest contribution to the daily business of caring for children and continue to do very little of the unpaid work in the home. If they are to take a more equal share in the care of children and in domestic work, massive changes in the structure of society, in particular the way in which childcare and work are organized, will have to occur to enable and support the change in men's attitudes that is also needed.

However, in considering the involvement of men in children's lives we should not assume that a male role model or father figure is necessary for so-called normal, healthy development. Another problem with the demand for shared parenting is that it could work against the struggle for better public provision for childcare. We need to insist on public responsibility for childcare, as we do for education of children after the age of five.

In considering what becoming and being a mother means to women, it is clear that we need to examine not only the social and material conditions in which women give birth to and rear children, but also the beliefs and expectations that they hold about reproduction and childrearing. Throughout this century opinion and advice towards mothers by, usually male, childcare 'experts' has played an important role in shaping such beliefs and expectations. In particular it has contributed to an idealized view of motherhood and the family which continues to be part of the official rhetoric of politicians and policy-makers.

As I have shown, it was in the fifties that this idealization of the mother reached a peak and, against this context, feminists in the sixties and early seventies sought to draw attention to those aspects of having and caring for children which were being ignored or denied, particularly the negative aspects. We still need to challenge the tendency to glorify and romanticise the family and motherhood, whilst ignoring the realities involved in caring for children. In Britain in the 80s the government was keen to emphasize the importance of family life and community care, yet it all-too-often failed to acknowledge that it is women's unpaid labour that allows this to occur and that the conditions in which this work is carried out are very often those of poverty and hardship.

In this book I have attempted to place motherhood in a social and political framework. In particular I have tried to test out some of the neglected questions and some of the contradictions in feminist thinking about reproduction and childrearing. Hopefully such questioning will help us to see more clearly how, as women, we ᴄ ᴀin more power and control over decisions about if, when exual activity takes place and, related to this, whether ᴠish to have children.

Bibliography

Antonis, Barbie (1981) 'Motherhood and Mothering' in *Women and Society*, The Cambridge Women's Studies Group, London, Virago, pp. 55–74.

Arcana, Judith (1981) *Our Mothers' Daughters*, London, Women's Press.

Arcana, Judith (1983) *Every Mother's Son*, London, Women's Press.

Arditti, Rita, Klein, Renate, Duelli and Minden, Shelley (eds) (1984) *Test Tube Women*, London, Pandora Press.

Badinter, Elisabeth (1981) *The Myth of Motherhood*, London, Souvenir Press.

Ballard, R. (1982) 'South Asian Families' in N. Rapaport, M. Fogarty and R. Rapaport (eds) *Families in Britain*, London, Routledge & Kegan Paul.

Banks, Olive (1981) *Faces of Feminism*, Oxford, Martin Robertson.

Beail, Nicholas and McGuire, Jamie (eds) (1982) *Fathers: Psychological Aspects*, London, Junction Books.

Beauvoir, Simone de, (1953) *The Second Sex*, London, Jonathan Cape.

Bhavnani, Kum-Kum and Coulson, Margaret (1986) 'Transforming Socialist Feminism: The Challenge of Racism', *Feminist Review*, no. 23.

Billings, Evelyn, L., Billings, John J. and Catarinich, Maurice (1974) *Atlas of the Ovulation Method*, Australia, Advocate Press.

Bilton, Tony, Bonnett, Kevin, Jones, Philip, Stanworth, Michelle, Sheard Ken and Webster, Andrew (eds) (1987) *Introductory Sociology*, 2nd edn, London, Macmillan.

Birke, Lynda, Himmelweit, Susan and Vines, Gail (eds) (1990) *Tomorrow's Child: Reproductive Technologies in the 90s*, London, Virago.

Boulton, Mary G. (1983) *On Being a Mother*, London, Tavistock Publications.

Bowlby, John (1951) *Maternal Care and Mental Health*, Geneva, World Health Organisation.

Bowlby, John (1953) *Child Care and the Growth of Love*, London, Penguin.

Boyle, M. (1992), 'The Abortion Debate,' in Paula Nicolson and Jane Ussher (eds), *The Psychology of Women's Health and Health Care*, London, Macmillan.

Breen, Dana (1975) *The Birth of a First Child*, London, Tavistock.

Brown, George and Harris, Tirril (1978) *Social Origins of Depression*, London, Tavistock.

Brown, George, Andrews, B., Harris, Tirril, Adler, Z. and Bridge, L. (1986) 'Social support, self-esteem and depression', *Psychological Medicine*, vol. 16, pp. 813–31.

Bryan, Beverley, Dadzie, Stella and Scafe, Suzanne (1985) *Heart of the Race*, London, Virago.

Cameron, Deborah (1990) *The Feminist Critique of Language*, London, Routledge.

Carmichael, E. (1977) *Non-Sexist Childraising*, Boston, Beacon Press.

Central Policy Review Staff (1978) *Services for Young Children With Working Mothers*, London, HMSO.

Central Statistical Office (CSO) (1989) *Social Trends*, London, HMSO.

Cherfas, Jeremy and Gribbin, John (1984) *The Redundant Male*, London, Bodley Head.

Chodorow, Nancy (1978) *The Reproduction of Mothering*, Berkeley, University of California Press.

Church, Joseph (1976) *Understanding Your Child From Birth To Three*, London, Fontana.

Comer, Lee (1982) 'Monogamy, marriage and economic independence' in Elizabeth Whitelegg *et al.* (eds), *The Changing Experience of Women*, Oxford, Martin Robertson, pp. 178–89.

Corea, Gena (1988) *The Mother Machine*, London, Women's Press.

Corea, Gena *et al.* (1985) *Man Made Women: How New Reproductive Technologies Affect Women*, London, Hutchinson.

Dally, Ann (1982) *Inventing Motherhood: The Consequences of an Ideal*, London, Burnett Books.

Daly, Mary (1979) *Gyn/Ecology*, London, The Women's Press.

Daly, Mary (1984) *Pure Lust*, London, The Women's Press.

Davidson, Hilda (1985) 'Unfriendly myths about women teachers', in Judith Whyte, Rosemary Deem, Lesley Kant and Maureen Cruikshank (eds), *Girl Friendly Schooling*, London, Methuen, pp. 191–208.

Davies, Martin (1981) *The Essential Social Worker*, London, Heinemann.

Dowrick, Stephanie and Grundberg, Sibyl (eds) (1980) *Why Children?* London, Women's Press.

Drake, Katia and Drake, Jonathan (1984) *Natural Birth Control*, Wellingborough, Thorsons.

Dworkin, Andrea (1983) *Right Wing Women*, London, The Women's Press.

Ehrenreich, Barbara and English, Deirdre (1979) *For Her Own Good: 150 Years of the Expert's Advice to Women*, London, Pluto Press.

Equal Opportunities Commission (1990) *Women and Men in Britain 1990*, London, HMSO.

Family Policy Studies Centre (FPSC) (1990) *Family Changes*, London.

Fidell, Linda, Hoffman, Donnie and Keith-Spiegel, Patti (1979) 'Some social implications of sex-choice technology', *Psychology of Women Quarterly*, vol. 4, no. 1, pp. 32–9.

Firestone, Shulamith (1971) *The Dialectic of Sex*, London, Jonathan Cape.

Friday, Nancy (1979) *My Mother My Self*, London, Fontana.

Friedan, Betty (1963) *The Feminine Mystique*, London, Gollancz.

Friedan, Betty (1981) *The Second Stage*, New York, Summit Books.

Fuller, Mary (1982) 'Young, Female and Black' in Ernest Cashmore and Barry Troyna (eds) *Black Youth in Crisis*, London, Routledge & Kegan Paul.

Gavron, Hannah (1966) *The Captive Wife: Conflicts of Housebound Mothers*, London, Penguin.

General Household Survey (GHS) (1989) London, OPCS, HMSO.

Gittins, Diana (1985) *The Family in Question*, London, Macmillan.

Golombok, Susan, Spencer, Ann and Rutter, Michael (1983) 'Children in lesbian and single-parent households: psychosexual and psychiatric appraisal', *Journal of Child Psychology and Psychiatry*, vol. 24, no. 4, pp. 551–72.

Gordon, Linda and DuBois, Ellen (1987) 'Seeking Ecstasy on the Battle-field: Danger and Pleasure in Nineteenth-Century Feminist Sexual Thought' in Feminist Review (eds), *Sexuality: A Reader*, London, Virago, pp. 82–97.

Gordon, Tuala (1990) *Feminist Mothers*, London, Macmillan.

Grabucker, Marianne (1988) *There's a Good Girl*, London, Women's Press.

Graham, Hilary (1982) 'Coping: or how mothers are seen and not heard', in Scarlet Friedman and Elizabeth Sarah (eds), *On the Problem of Men*, London, Women's Press, pp. 101–116.

Graham, Hilary (1987) 'Women's Poverty and Caring', in C. Glendinning and J. Millar (eds), *Women and Poverty in Britain*, Brighton, Wheat-sheaf, pp. 221–40.

Green, Richard (1978) 'Sexual identity of 37 children raised by homo-sexual or trans-sexual parents', *American Journal of Psychiatry*, vol. 135, pp. 692–7.

Greer, Germaine (1984) *Sex and Destiny*, London, Secker & Warburg.

Griffin, Chris (1986) 'Qualitative Methods and Female Experience: Young Women From School to the Job Market', in Sue Wilkinson (ed.), *Feminist Social Psychology: Developing Theory and Practice*, Milton Keynes, Open University Press.

Griffin, Susan (1981) *Woman and Nature*, London, The Women's Press.

Hall, Radclyffe (1981) *The Unlit Lamp*, London, Virago.

Halson, Jacqui (1989) 'The sexual harassment of young women', in Lesley Holly (ed.), *Girls and Sexuality*, Milton Keynes, Open University Press, pp. 130–42.

Hamblin, Angela (1982) 'What can one do with a son? Feminist politics and male children', in Scarlet Friedman and Elizabeth Sarah (eds), *On The Problem of Men*, London, Women's Press, pp. 238–44.

Hanmer, Jalna (1981) 'Sex predetermination, artificial insemination and the maintenance of male-dominated culture', in Helen Roberts (ed.),

Women, Health and Reproduction, London, Routledge & Kegan Paul, pp. 163–90.

Hanmer, Jalna (1992) 'Women and Reproduction', in Diane Richardson and Victoria Robinson (eds): *Introducing Women's Studies: Feminist Theory and Practice*, London, Macmillan.

Hardyment, Christina (1983) *Dream Babies: Childcare from Locke to Spock*, London, Cape.

Hemmings, Susan (1980) 'Horrific practices: How lesbians were presented in newspapers of 1978', in Gay Left Collective (ed.), *Homosexuality: Power and Politics*, London, Allison and Busby, pp. 157–71.

Hewlett, Sylvia (1987) *A Lesser Life: The Myth of Women's Liberation*, London, Michael Joseph.

hooks, bell (1982) *Ain't I a Woman: Black Women and Feminism*, London, Pluto Press.

ILA (1989), *IVF Research in the U.K.: A Report on Research Licensed by the Interim Licensing Authority (ILA) for Human In Vitro Fertilisation and Embryology 1985–1989*, London, ILA.

Jackson, Stevi (1992) 'Women and the Family', in Diane Richardson and Victoria Robinson (eds): *Introducing Women's Studies: Feminist Theory and Practice*, London, Macmillan.

Jeffreys, Sheila (1985) *The Spinster and Her Enemies*, London, Pandora Press.

Jolly, Hugh (1975) *Book of Child Care*, London, Allen & Unwin (revised edition, 1986).

Jones, Carole (1985) 'Sexual tyranny: Male violence in a mixed secondary school', in Gaby Weiner (ed.), *Just a Bunch of Girls: Feminist approaches to schooling*, Milton Keynes, Open University Press.

Kaye, Kenneth (1977) 'Toward the origin of dialogue', in H. Rudolph Schaffer (ed.), *Studies in Mother-Infant Interaction*, London, Academic Press, pp. 89–117.

Kidd, Tony (1982) 'Social security and the family', in Ivan Reid and Eileen Wormald (eds), *Sex Differences in Britain*, London, Grant McIntyre, pp. 59–84.

Kishwar, Madhu (1985) 'The continuing deficit of women in India and the impact of amniocentesis', in Gena Corea *et al.* (eds), *Man made Women*, London, Hutchinson, pp. 30–37.

Klein, Renate D. (1984) 'Doing it ourselves', in Rita Arditti, Renate D. Klein and Shelley Minden (eds), *Test Tube Women*, London, Pandora Press, pp. 382–8.

Klein, Renate D. (ed.) (1989) *Infertility: Women speak out about their experiences of reproductive medicine*, London, Pandora Press.

Lamb, Michael E. (ed.) (1981) *The Role of the Father in Child Development*, 2nd ed, New York, Wiley & Sons.

Land, Hilary (1976) 'Women: Supporters or supported?', in Diana Leonard Barker and Sheila Allen (eds), *Sexual Divisions in Society*, London, Tavistock, pp. 108–132.

Land, Hilary (1982) 'The family wage', in Mary Evans (ed.), *The Woman Question*, London, Fontana, pp. 289–96.

Leach, Penelope (1984) *Baby and Child*, London, Penguin (first published in 1977).

Lees, Sue (1986) *Losing Out*, London, Hutchinson.

Lewis, Charlie and O'Brien, Margaret (eds) (1987) *Reassessing Fatherhood*, London, Sage.

Lewis, Jane (1984) *Women in England 1870–1950: Sexual Divisions and Social Change*, Sussex, Wheatsheaf Books.

Liddiard, Mabel (1954) *The Mothercraft Manual*, 12th edn, London, Churchill.

Llewellyn Davis, Margaret (1978) *Maternity, Letters from Working Women*, London, Virago (first published in 1915).

Lomax, Elizabeth M. R. (1978) *Science and Patterns of Child Care*, London, W. H. Freeman & Co.

Macintyre, Sally (1976) 'Who Wants Babies? The social construction of instincts', in Diana Leonard Barker and Sheila Allen (eds), *Sexual Divisions and Society: Process and Change*, London, Tavistock, pp. 150–73.

Mahony, Pat (1985) *Schools for the Boys? Co-education Reassessed*, London, Hutchinson.

Martin, J. and Roberts, C. (1984) *Women and Employment*, Department of Employment/OPCS, HMSO.

McKee, Lorna and Bell, C. (1985) 'His unemployment: her problem. The domestic and marital consequences of male unemployment', in S. Allen *et al.* (eds), London, Macmillan.

McKee, Lorna and O'Brien, Margaret (eds) (1982) *The Father Figure*, London, Tavistock.

Mead, Margaret (1954) 'Some theoretical considerations of the problem of mother-child separation', *American Journal of Orthopsychiatry*, vol. 24, pp. 471–83.

Mitchell, Juliet (1971) *Women's Estate*, London, Penguin.

Mitchell, Juliet (1974) *Psychoanalysis and Feminism*, London, Allen Lane.

Moncrieff, Alan (1948) *Practical Motherhood and Parentcraft*, London, Oldhams Press.

Morris, Norman (ed.) (1983) *The Baby Book*, London, Newbourne.

Newson, John (1979) 'The growth of shared understandings between infant and care giver', in Margaret Bullowa (ed.), *Before Speech: The beginnings of interpersonal communication*, London, Cambridge University Press, pp. 207–22.

Newson, John and Newson, Elizabeth (1974) 'Cultural aspects of child-rearing in the English-speaking world', in Martin P. M. Richards (ed.), *The Integration of a Child into a Social World*, London, Cambridge University Press, pp. 53–82.

Nicholson, Joyce (1983) *The Heartache of Motherhood*, London, Sheldon Press.

Oakley, Ann (1974) *The Sociology of Housework*, Oxford, Martin Robertson.

Oakley, Ann (1979) *Becoming a Mother*, Oxford, Martin Robertson.

Oakley, Ann (1980) *Women Confined*, Oxford, Martin Robinson.

Oakley, Ann (1981) *Subject Women*, Oxford, Martin Robertson.

Office of Population and Census Survey (OPCS) (1990), London, HMSO.

Palmer, Gabrielle (1988) *The Politics of Breastfeeding*, London, Pandora Press.

Park, Christine and Heaton, C. (eds) (1987) *Close Company: Stories of Mothers and Daughters*, London, Virago.

Parke, Ross D. (1981) *Fathering*, London, Fontana.

Pfeffer, Naomi and Woollett, Anne (1983) *The Experience of Infertility*, London, Virago.

Phoenix, Ann (1991) *Young Mothers?* London, Polity Press.

Piachaud, David (1984) *Round About Fifty Hours a Week*, London, Child Poverty Action Group.

Pilling, Doria and Pringle, Mia Kellmer (1978) *Controversial Issues in Child Development*, London, Paul Elek.

Pollock, Scarlet and Sutton, Jo (1987) *The Politics of Fatherhood*, London, Women's Press.

Pugh, Gillian (ed.) (1980) *Preparation for Parenthood*, London, National Children's Bureau.

Radford, Jill (1991) 'Immaculate Conceptions', *Trouble and Strife*, no. 21, pp. 8–12.

Rakusen, Jill (1981) 'Depo-Provera: the extent of the problem. A case study in the politics of birth control', in Helen Roberts (ed.), *Women, Health and Reproduction*, London, Routledge & Kegan Paul, pp. 75–108.

Rand, C., Graham, D. L. R. and Rawlings, E. I. (1982) 'Psychological health and factors the court seeks to control in lesbian mother custody trials', *Journal of Homosexuality*, vol. 8, no. 1, pp. 27–39.

Renvoize, Jean (1985) *Going Solo: Single Mothers by Choice*, London, Routledge & Kegan Paul.

Rich, Adrienne (1976) *Of Woman Born*, New York, W.W. Norton & Co.

Richardson, Diane (1981a) 'Lesbian mothers', in John Hart and Diane Richardson, *The Theory and Practice of Homosexuality*, London, Routledge & Kegan Paul, pp. 149–58.

Richardson, Diane (1981b) 'Theoretical perspectives on homosexuality', in John Hart and Diane Richardson, *The Theory and Practice of Homosexuality*, London, Routledge & Kegan Paul, pp. 5–37.

Richardson, Diane (1984) 'The dilemma of essentiality in homosexual theory', *Journal of Homosexuality*, vol. 9, no. 2/3, pp. 79–90.

Richardson, Diane (1989) *Women and the AIDS Crisis*, 2nd edn, London, Pandora Press.

Rights of Women Lesbian Custody Group (1986) *Lesbian Mothers Legal Handbook*, London, Women's Press.

Riley, Denise (1983a) *War in the Nursery: Theories of the Child and Mother*, London, Virago.

Riley, Denise (1983b) 'The Serious Burdens of Love? Some Questions on Child-care, Feminism and Socialism', in Lynne Segal (ed.), *What is to be done about the family?* Harmondsworth, Penguin, pp. 129–56.

Roberts, Helen (1981) 'Male hegemony in family planning', in Helen Roberts (ed.), *Women, Health and Reproduction*, London, Routledge & Kegan Paul, pp. 1–17.

Rorvik, D and Shettles, L. (1977) *Choose Your Baby's Sex*, New York, Dodd, Mead.

Rose, Hilary (1987) 'Victorian Values in the Test-Tube: the Politics of Reproductive Science and Technology', in Michelle Stanworth (ed.), *Reproductive Technologies*, London, Polity Press, pp. 151–73.

Rose, Hilary and Hanmer, Jalna (1976) 'Women's liberation, reproduction and the technological fix', in Diana Leonard Baker and Sheila Allen (eds), *Sexual Divisions and Society: Process and Change*, London, Tavistock, pp. 199–223.

Rossi, Alice (1977) 'A biosocial perspective on parenting', *Daedalus*, no. 106, pp. 1–32.

Russell, Graeme (1983) *The Changing Role of Fathers*, Milton Keynes, Open University Press.

Rutter, Michael (1981) *Maternal Deprivation Reassessed*, 2nd edn, London, Penguin.

Saffron, Lisa (1987) *Getting Pregnant Our Own Way: A Guide to Alternative Insemination* (second edition) London, Women's Health Information Centre.

Sayers, Janet (1982) *Biological Politics: Feminist and Anti-Feminist Perspectives*, London, Tavistock.

Schaffer, Rudolph, H. (1977a) *Mothering*, London, Fontana.

Schaffer, Rudolph, H. (1977b) 'Early interactive development', in H. Rudolph Schaffer (ed.) *Studies in Mother-Infant Interaction*, London, Academic Press, pp. 3–16.

Segal, Lynne (1987) *Is the future female?* London, Virago.

Shapiro, Jean (1987) *A Child: Your Choice*, London, Pandora Press.

Sharpe, Sue (1976) *Just Like a Girl: How Girls Learn to be Women*, Harmondsworth, Pelican.

Sharpe, Sue (1984) *Double Identity: the lives of working mothers*, Harmondsworth, Penguin.

Singer, Peter and Wells, Deane (1984) *The Reproduction Revolution, New Ways of Making Babies*, Oxford University Press.

Skeates, Jane and Jabri, Dorian (1988) *Fostering and Adoption by Lesbians and Gay Men*, London, London Strategic Policy Unit.

Sluckin, William, Herbert, Martin and Herbert, A. (1983) *Maternal Bonding*, London, Grant McIntyre.

Spender, Dale (1980) *Man Made Language*, London, Routledge & Kegan Paul.

Spock, Benjamin (1946/1973) *Baby and Child Care*, New York, Duell, Sloan and Pearce.

Spock, Benjamin (1974) *Bringing Up Children in a Difficult Time*, London, Bodley Head.

Stacey, Margaret (1981) 'The division of labour revisited or overcoming the two Adams', in Abrams *et al.* (eds), *Practice and Progress: British Sociology 1950–1980*, London, George Allen and Unwin.

Stanworth, Michelle (ed.) (1987) *Reproductive Technologies: Gender, Motherhood and Medicine*, London, Polity Press.

Statham, June (1986) *Non-Sexist Child Raising*, London, Blackwell.

Steedman, J. (1983) *Examination Results in Mixed and Single-Sex Schools: Findings from the National Child Development Study*, Manchester, Equal Opportunities Commission.

Stein, Sara (1984) *Girls and Boys: The Limits of Non-sexist Childrearing*, London, Chatto and Windus.

Stern, Daniel (1977) *The First Relationship: Infant and Mother*, London, Fontana.

Stoppard, Miriam (1984) *The Babycare Book*, London, Dorling Kindersley.

Sutton, Jo and Friedman, Scarlet (1982) 'Fatherhood: Bringing it all back home', in Scarlet Friedman and Elizabeth Sarah (eds), *On the Problem of Men*, London, The Women's Press, pp. 117–27.

Trevarthen, Colwyn (1979) 'Communication and cooperation in early infancy: a description of primary intersubjectivity', in Margaret Bullowa (ed.), *Before Speech: The Beginning of Interpersonal Communication*, London, Cambridge University Press, pp. 321–47.

United States Children's Bureau (1973) *Infant Care*, Washington DC, United States Government Printing Office (originally published 1914; revised and republished, 1921, 1942, 1951).

Walvin, James (1982) *A Child's World: A Social History of English Childhood, 1800–1914*, London, Penguin.

Warnock, Mary (1984) *The Report of the Committee of Inquiry into Human Fertilization and Embryology*, London, HMSO.

Watson, John B. (1928) *Psychological Care of Infant and Child*, New York, W. W. Norton & Co.

Weeks, Jeffrey (1986) *Sexuality*, London, Tavistock.

Weeks, Jeffrey (1990) *Sex, Politics and Society*, 2nd edn, London, Longman.

Weiss, Nancy Pottishman (1978) 'The mother-child dyad revisited: Perceptions of mothers and children in twentieth century childrearing manuals', *Journal of Social Issues*, vol. 34, no. 2, pp. 29–45.

White, James *et al.* (1978) *A Bill to remove the legal disabilities of children born out of wedlock*, London, HMSO.

Whyld, Janie (ed.) (1983) *Sexism in the Secondary Curriculum*, London, Harper & Row.

Will, Jerri, Self, Patricia and Datan, Nancy (1974) unpublished paper presented at 82nd annual meeting of the American Psychological Association.

Wilson, Elizabeth (1977) *Women and the Welfare State*, London, Tavistock.

Wilson, Elizabeth (1980) *Only Halfway to Paradise*, London, Tavistock.

Winnicott, Donald W. (1964) *The Child, the Family, and the Outside World*, London, Penguin.

Wolfenstein, Martha (1955) 'Fun morality: An analysis of recent American child-training literature', in Margaret Mead and Martha Wolfenstein (eds), *Childhood in Contemporary Cultures*, Chicago, University of Chicago Press, pp. 168–78.

Women's Reproductive Rights Information Centre (WRRIC) *Newsletter*, October–December 1987, London.

Young, Michael and Willmott, Peter (1973) *The Symmetrical Family*, London, Routledge & Kegan Paul.

Index